KNITTING AT Home

Knitting Patterns Inspired by the Indie Dyers of Oregon

THERESSA SILVER

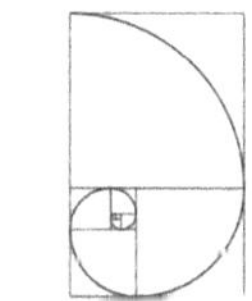

Theressa J. Silver Press
Oregon

Knitting at Home

ISBN-13: 978-1-7335704-3-5
First Edition
Published by Theressa J. Silver Press

Copy Editor: Stephen B. Gerken

Test Knitters:
Marilyn Barnes
Su Fennern
Heather Hagen
Kendra Meinert Hodson
Barbara Holland
Jan Just
Michele A. Ray
Dawn Rosiejka
Eva Schweber
Renata Suzuki
Margaret Weddell
Kim Williams

Every effort has been made to ensure that all the information in this book is accurate at the time of publication. However, Theressa J. Silver Press neither endorses nor guarantees the content of external links referenced in this book.

If you have questions or comments about this book, or need information about licensing, custom editions, special sales, or academic/corporate purchases, please contact Theressa J. Silver Press: tsilver@spiretech.com

This book is dedicated to
Diana McIntosh.
Thank you for opening your home and
your heart to me.

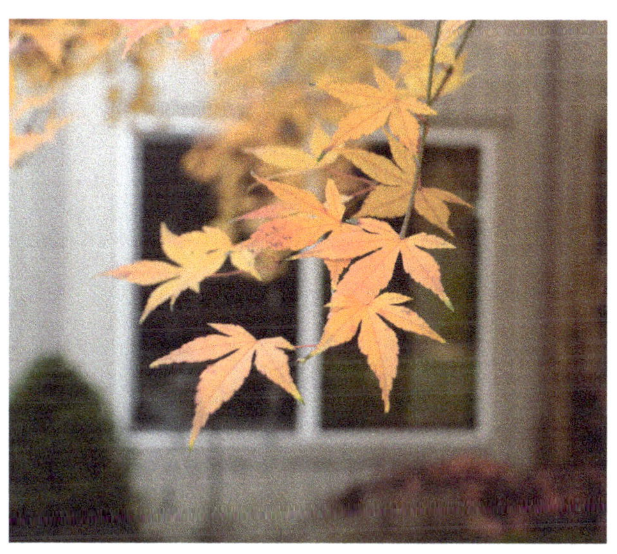

Patterns

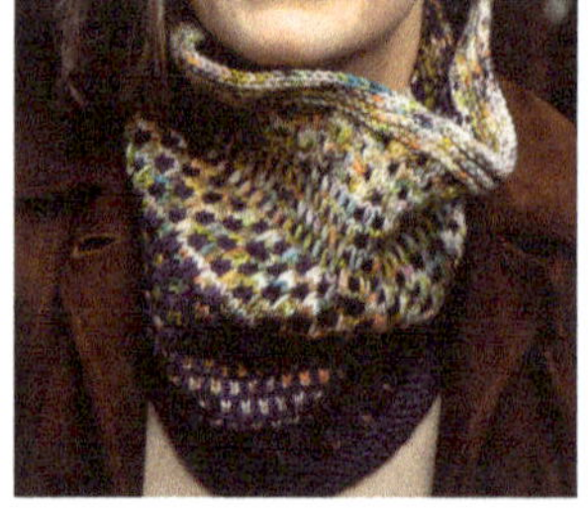

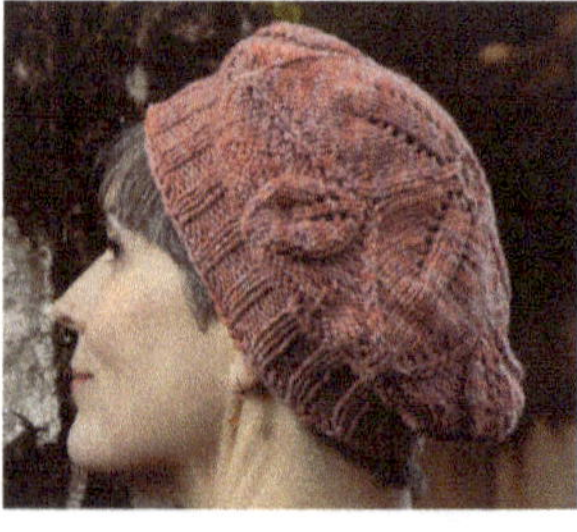

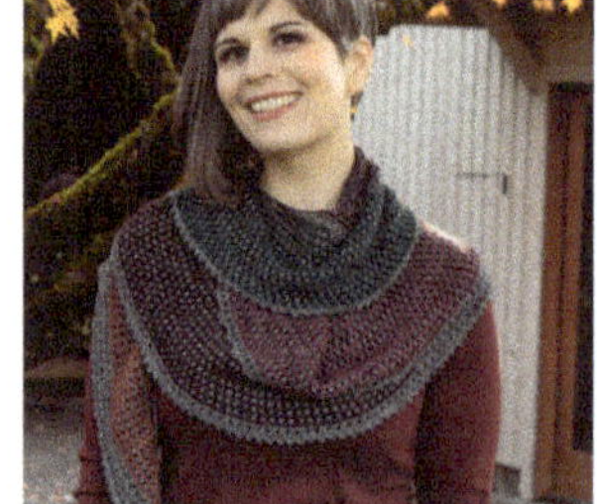

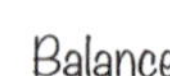

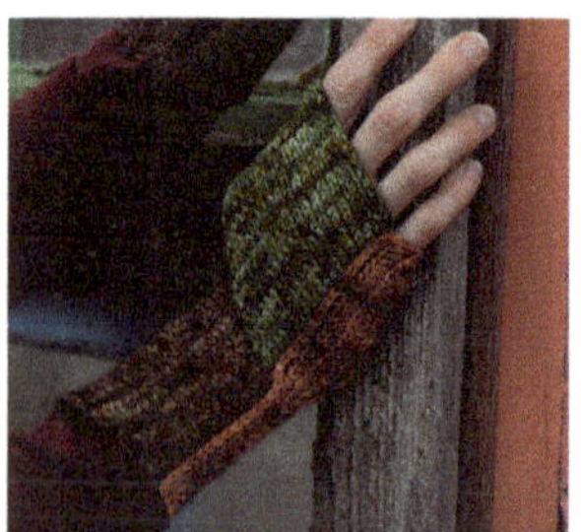

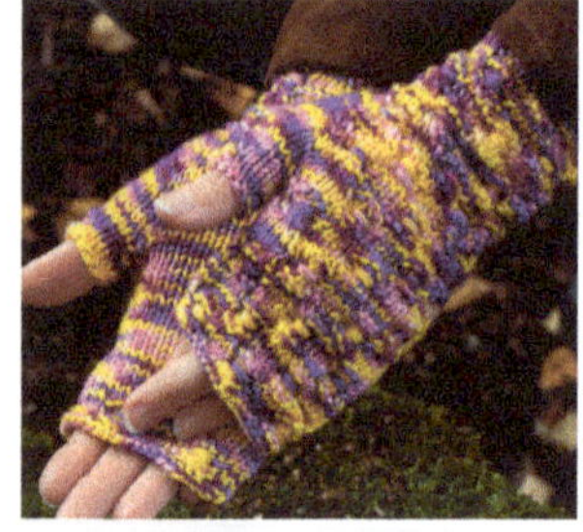

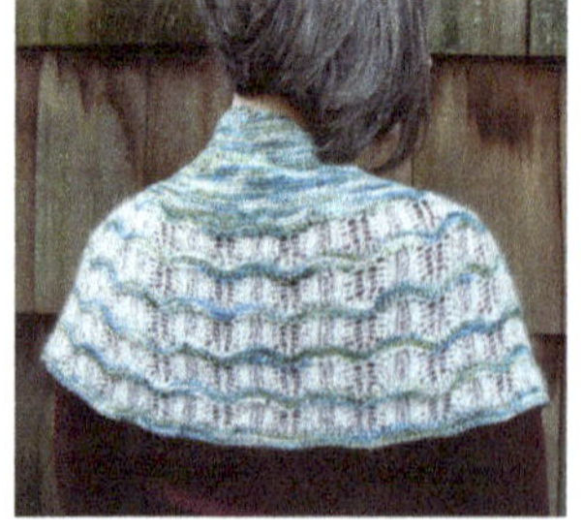

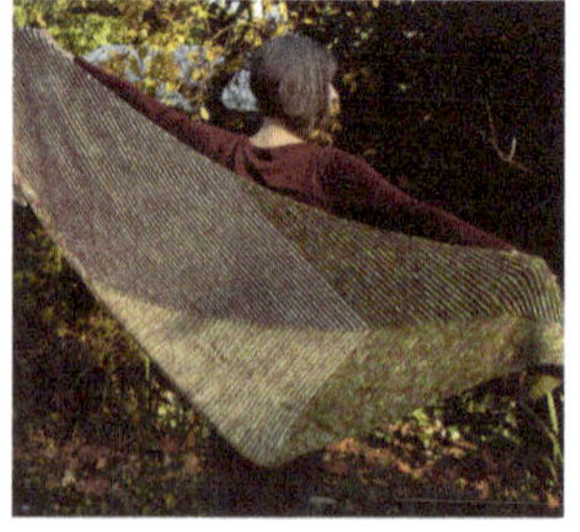

Introduction

On March 17, 2020, Oregon Governor Kate Brown issued the shelter in place order and Oregon shut down. We stayed home and we stayed safe. But that didn't mean we did nothing. Quite the contrary. We began exploring what was right around us. People gardened, and baked, and took up crafts. We learned new ways of interacting with friends and reached out to our communities for support. I turned to my knitting and found myself deeply inspired to create projects that reflected the idea of staying close to home.

I decided to create a collection of patterns that was all about home, starting with the yarn itself. I reached out to indie dyers all over Oregon and the response was wonderful. I asked each dyer to tell me about herself, her business, her inspirations, and her life. Those conversations became the inspirations for each pattern. These patterns really are about the yarn and the women who create it.

In this book you'll meet well known dyers and dyers who are just getting started. The result is 11 patterns that reflect the diversity and creativity of the fiber community in Oregon.

List of Dyers

Abbreviations

BO	bind off
br4st dec	brioche 4 st decrease
br4st inc	brioche 4 st increase
brk	brioche knit
brp	brioche purl
CC	contrast color
cdd	central double decrease
CN	cable needle
CO	cast on
decr	decrease
incr	increase
k	knit
k2tog	knit 2 together
kfb	knit front back
kyok	knit, yarn over, knit
lcp	left cross purl
LH	left hand
lk	long knit
m1	make one
MC	main color

p	purl
p2tog	purl 2 together
p3tog	purl 3 together
pm	place marker
rcp	right cross purl
rep(s)	repeat(s)
RH	right hand
rnd	round
RS	right side
sl	slip
sl1yo	slip 1 yarn over
sm	slip marker
ssk	slip, slip, knit
sssk	slip, slip, slip, knit
st(s)	stitch(es)
tbl	through the back loop
WS	wrong side
wyib	with yarn in back
wyif	with yarn in front
yo	yarn over

Knitted Wit

Portland, OR

What began in a backyard in Portland, Oregon in 2007 has grown into a vibrant and socially-conscious dye house with a committed staff, a fearless (and multiple-print-wearing) leader, and just enough chocolate to help carry us through it all. Knitted Wit loves creating bright new colors, including a huge rainbow of semi-solids; a menagerie of colorways inspired by magical creatures; a colorful tour through the National Parks of the USA; and many Colorways for a Cause, raising funds and awareness for issues that strike a chord with us. We dig collaborating with other crafty folk all over the world, and love being a part of this craft community.

Website: www.knittedwit.com
Shop: www.etsy.com/shop/knittedwit
Instagram: @knittedwit
Email: hello@knittedwit.com
Our Community: forms.gle/8tXnm91BbvyMmKmD9

Reading the Knitted Wit blog (knittedwit.com/blog), I quickly realized that they are about inclusivity and collaboration and that their success stems from a successful blending of different personalities and skills. I wanted to bring this idea of equality and blending into my design. The "Better Together" cowl uses two contrasting yarns blending one into the other. Both yarns are used equally, but they take turns at center stage. While one is in the foreground the other is supporting from the background. The result is one harmonious whole in which each yarn shines brighter than it would on its own.

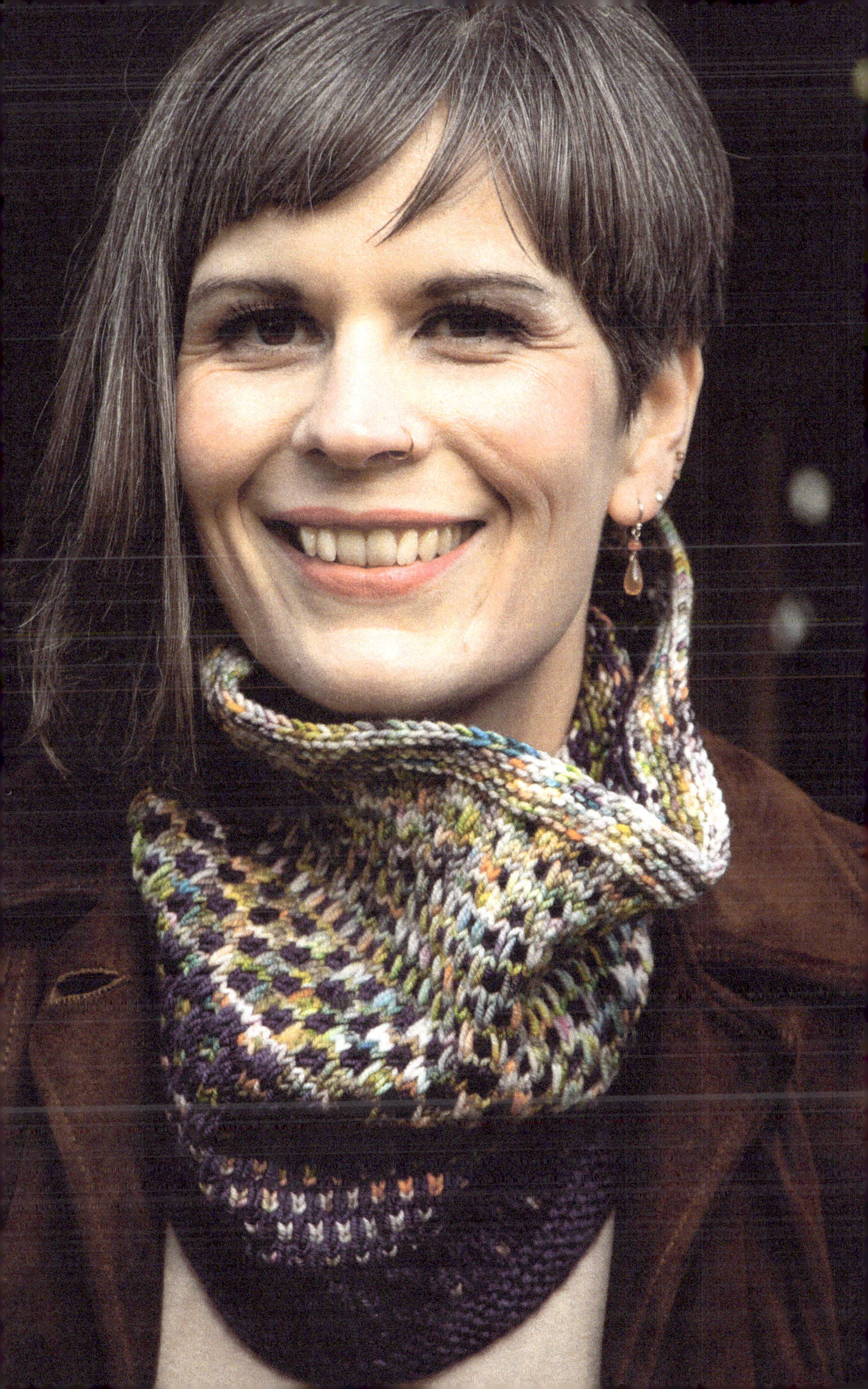

Better Together

Finished Measurments
Circumference: 23 inches / 58cm
Height: 11 inches / 28cm

Yarn
140 yards / 128m each of two colors of DK weight yarn

Yarn provided by Knitted Wit
DK: 100% superwash merino
280 yards per 4 ounces
Colorways: Hyacinth (solid) and Acadia National Park (variegated)

Other Materials
US size 6 (4mm) 24 inch / 60cm circular needles or size needed to obtain gauge

Stitch markers

Tapestry needle

Gauge
23 sts = 4 inches / 10cm in garter stitch

Pattern Note
Be sure to leave enough slack in the working yarn when slipping sts so as not to constrict the fabric.

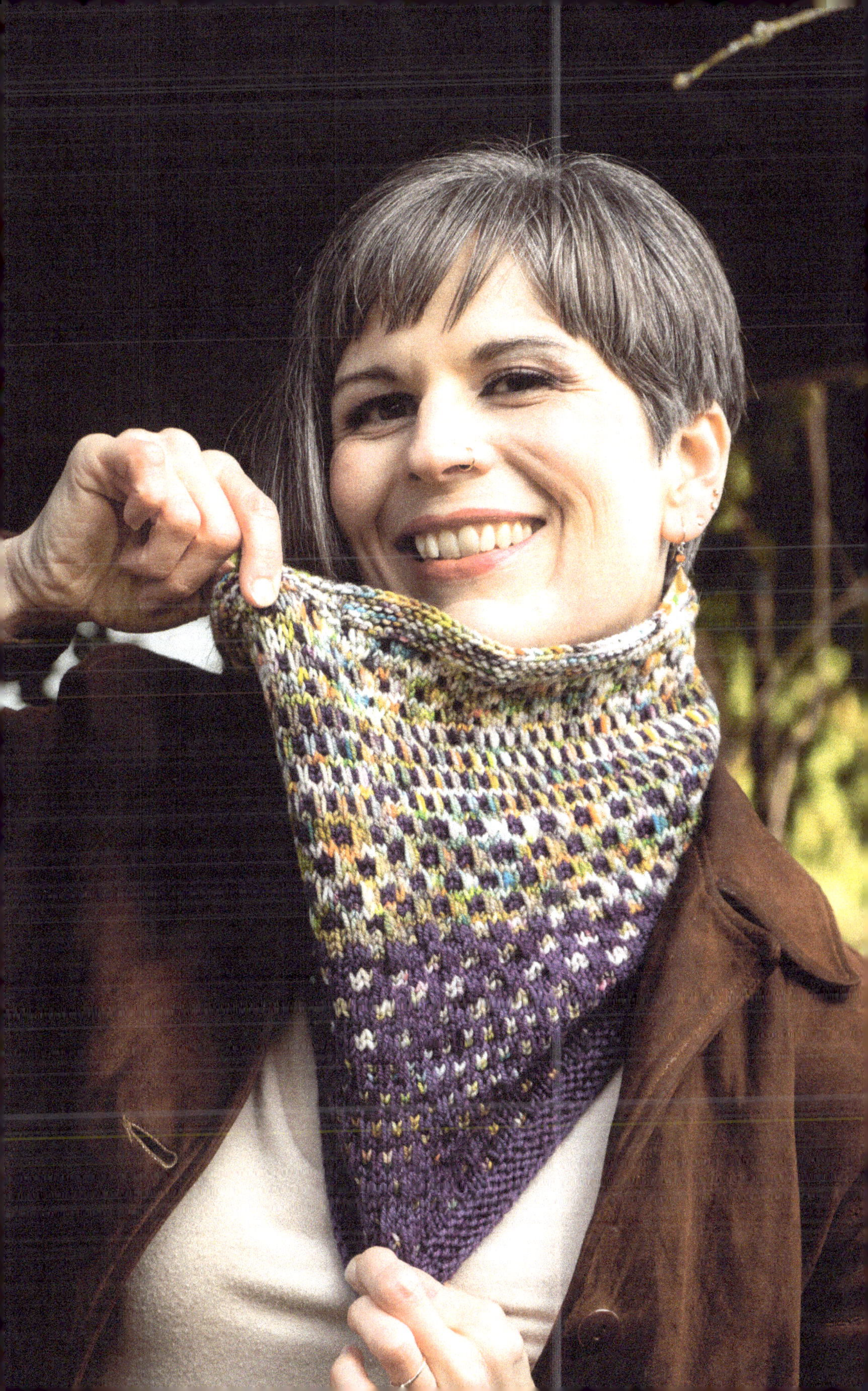

With color A, CO 132 sts and join in the round taking care not to twist the work. Place a marker for the end of the round.
Rnds 1, 3, and 5: Knit.
Rnds 2, 4, and 6: Purl.

Rnds 7 and 8: With color A, knit.
Rnds 9 and 10: With color B, *k1, sl3, rep from * to end of rnd.
Rnds 11 and 12: With color A, knit.
Rnds 13 and 14: With color B, sl2, *k1, sl3, rep from * to the last st, sl1.
Rep rnds 7 - 14 once more (two reps total). Add another rep here if you want a taller cowl.

Rnds 15 and 16: With color A, knit.
Rnds 17 and 18: With color B, *sl1, k1, rep from * to end of rnd.
Rnds 19 and 20: With color A, knit.
Rnds 21 and 22: With color B, *k1, sl1, rep from * to the last st, sl1.
Rep rnds 15 - 22 once more (two reps total).

Rnds 23 and 24: With color A, knit.
Rnds 25 and 26: With color B, *k2, sl2, rep from * to end of rnd.
Rnds 27 and 28: With color A, knit.
Rnds 29 and 30: With color B, *sl2, k2, rep from * to the last st, sl1.
Rep rnds 23 - 30 once more (two reps total).

NOTE the color changes in the next section.
Rnds 31 and 32: With color B, knit.
Rnds 33 and 34: With color A, *sl2, k2, rep from * to end of rnd.
Rnds 35 and 36: With color B, knit.
Rnds 37 and 38: With color A, *k2, sl2, rep from * to the last st, sl1.
Rep rnds 31 - 38 once more (two reps total).

Rnds 39 and 40: With color B, knit.
Rnds 41 and 42: With color A, *sl1, k1, rep from * to end of rnd.
Rnds 43 and 44: With color B, knit.
Rnds 45 and 46: With color A, *k1, sl1, rep from * to the last st, sl1.
Rep rnds 39 - 46 once more (two reps total).

Rnds 47 and 48: With color B, knit.
Rnds 49 and 50: With color A, sl1, *k1, sl3, rep from * to the last st, sl2.
Rnds 51 and 52: With color B, knit.
Rnds 53 and 54: With color A, *sl3, k1, rep from * to end of rnd.

Rep rnds 47 - 54 once more (two reps total). Add another rep here if you want a taller cowl.

With color B:
Rnds 55 and 56: Knit
Rnds 57, 59, and 61: Purl.
Rnds 58, 60, and 62: Knitl.
BO all sts loosely.
Weave in ends and block to shape.

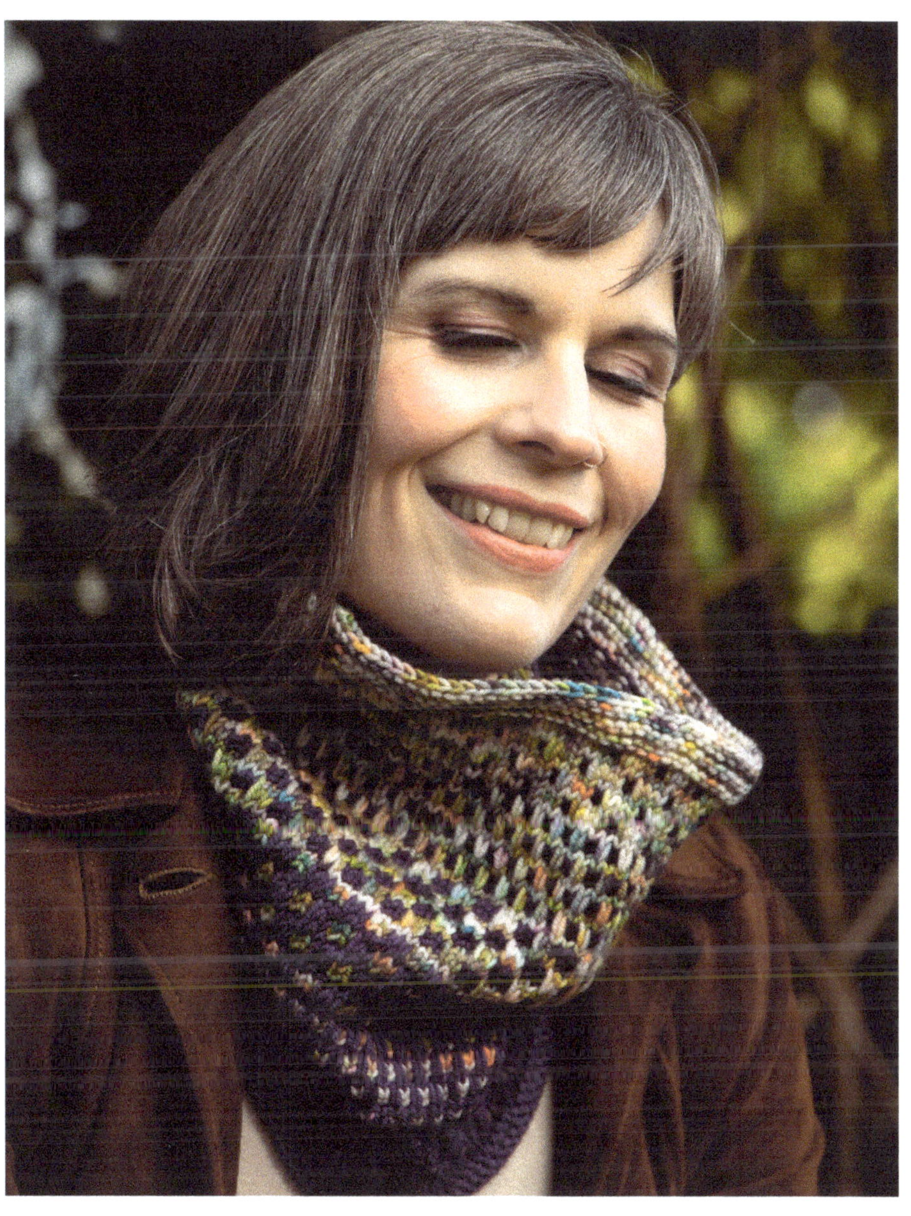

Siren Yarn Co.

Seaside, OR

Siren Yarn Co. is a collaboration between sisters Sarah Ehle and Allie Kloster. This creative duo hand-dyes yarn inspired by color and texture, beauty in nature, and the adventures in sisterhood.

Allie owns and manages Seaside Yarn and Fiber in Seaside, Oregon, and started dyeing yarn so she could offer something special to her customers. After seeing the positive response from the yarn community (and discovering how much fun it was) she asked her sister Sarah to join her.

Allie describes herself as a crafts person, while Sarah has degrees in Fine Arts and Art Therapy. Their collaboration between art and craft has produced a wonderful array of hand dyed yarns. Everyone has a different eye for color so it's fun to see what new colorways each sister comes up with.

Website: www.sirenyarn.com
Shop: www.seasideyarnandfiber.com
Instagram: @sirenyarnco
         @seasideyarnandfiber
Email: seasideyarnandfiber@gmail.com

I met Allie when she hosted me at Seaside Yarn and Fiber for a book signing and trunk show. I had a great time seeing her shop and meeting her customers. At the end of my visit she gifted me a skein of her beautiful naturally dyed Donegal DK. I spent the rest of the weekend on vacation with my husband. The weather and tides were perfect for beachcombing and we came home with a nice collection of shells and agates after a lovely weekend at the beach. The Beachcomber hat combines the soft ocean color of Allie's Indigo dyed yarn with the romance of a walk on the beach with someone you love.

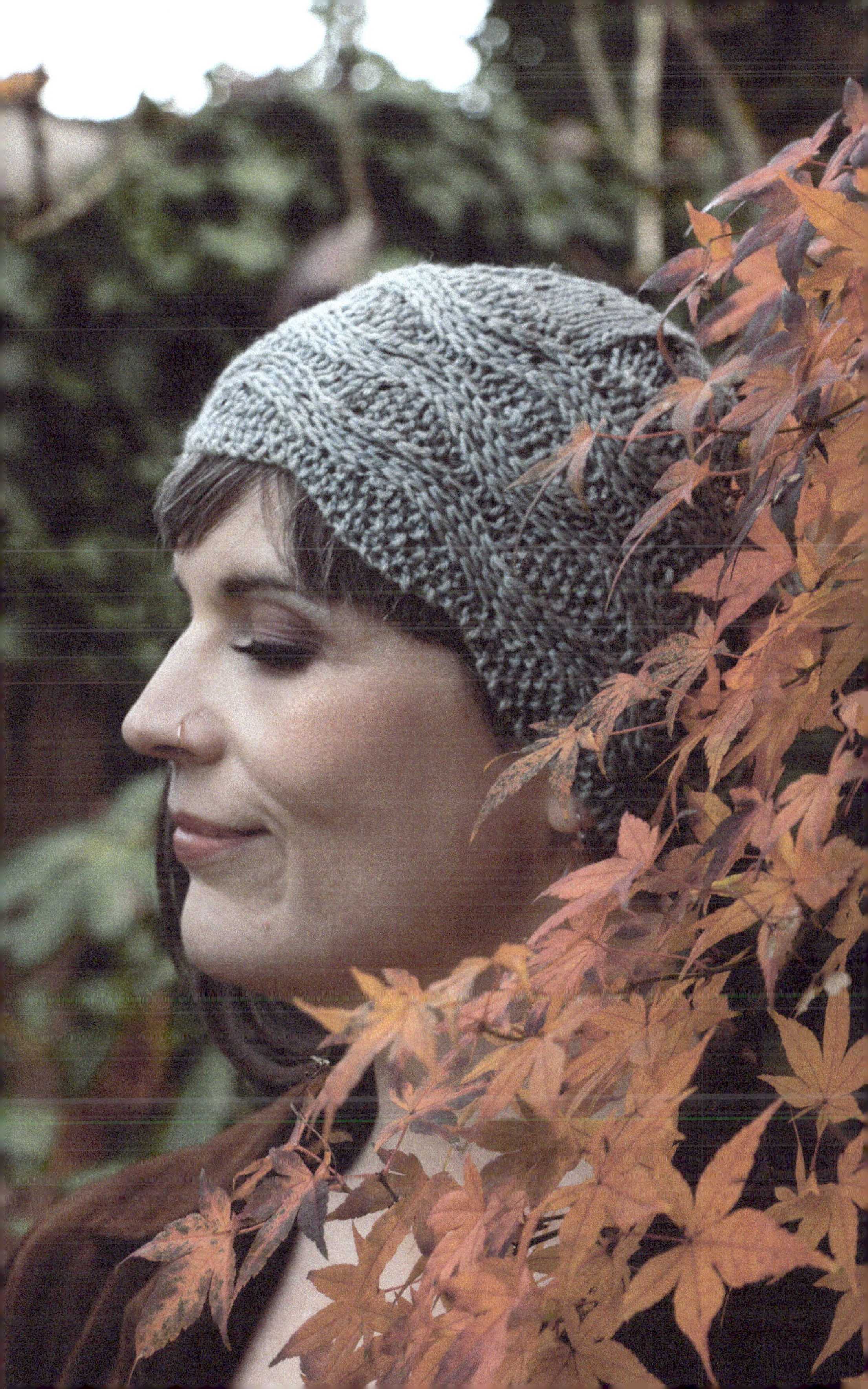

Beachcomber

SIZES
Small [Large] (shown in size small)
Fits head circumference 19 - 21 [22 - 24] inches / 48 - 54 [55 - 61] cm

YARN
75 yards / 70m of DK weight yarn
Note: An all or mostly wool yarn is preferable for structure since there is no ribbing at the brim of this hat.

Yarn provided by Siren Yarn Co.
Donegal DK: 85% superwash merino, 15% donegal nep
230 yards per 100g
Colorway: Indigo

OTHER MATERIALS
US size 8 (5mm) 40 inch / 100cm circular needle, or size needed to obtain gauge. This needle is used for both working flat and in the round using magic loop. A set of double pointed needles can be used instead for working in the round if preferred.

Tapestry needle

GAUGE
Row gauge matters for the fit of this hat and is best measured in the actual band pattern. Cast on and knit 2 reps of the band section. Leave the work on the needle and block gently. The piece should be 5 inches / 12.5cm long.

OR approximate at 32 ROWS = 4 inches / 10cm in seed stitch

PATTERN NOTE
Slip all sts with yarn in front.

PATTERN

Band (worked flat)

CO 28 sts. (Use a provisional cast on if you prefer to graft rather than seam the band.)

The following 20 rows are also presented in the waves chart if a chart is preferred.

Row 1 (RS): [K1, p1] twice, k1, m1, [k1, p1] twice, ssk, p1, k1, k2tog, [p1, k1] twice, m1, p1, k1, m1, [k1, p1] twice, ssk, k1.

Row 2 (WS): P1, [sl1, k1] twice, sl1, [p1, k1] twice, [sl1, k1] three times, p1, [sl1, k1] twice, sl1, [p1, k1] three times.

Row 3: [k1, p1] six times, k2tog, [p1, k1] twice, m1, [k1, p1] four times, k2.

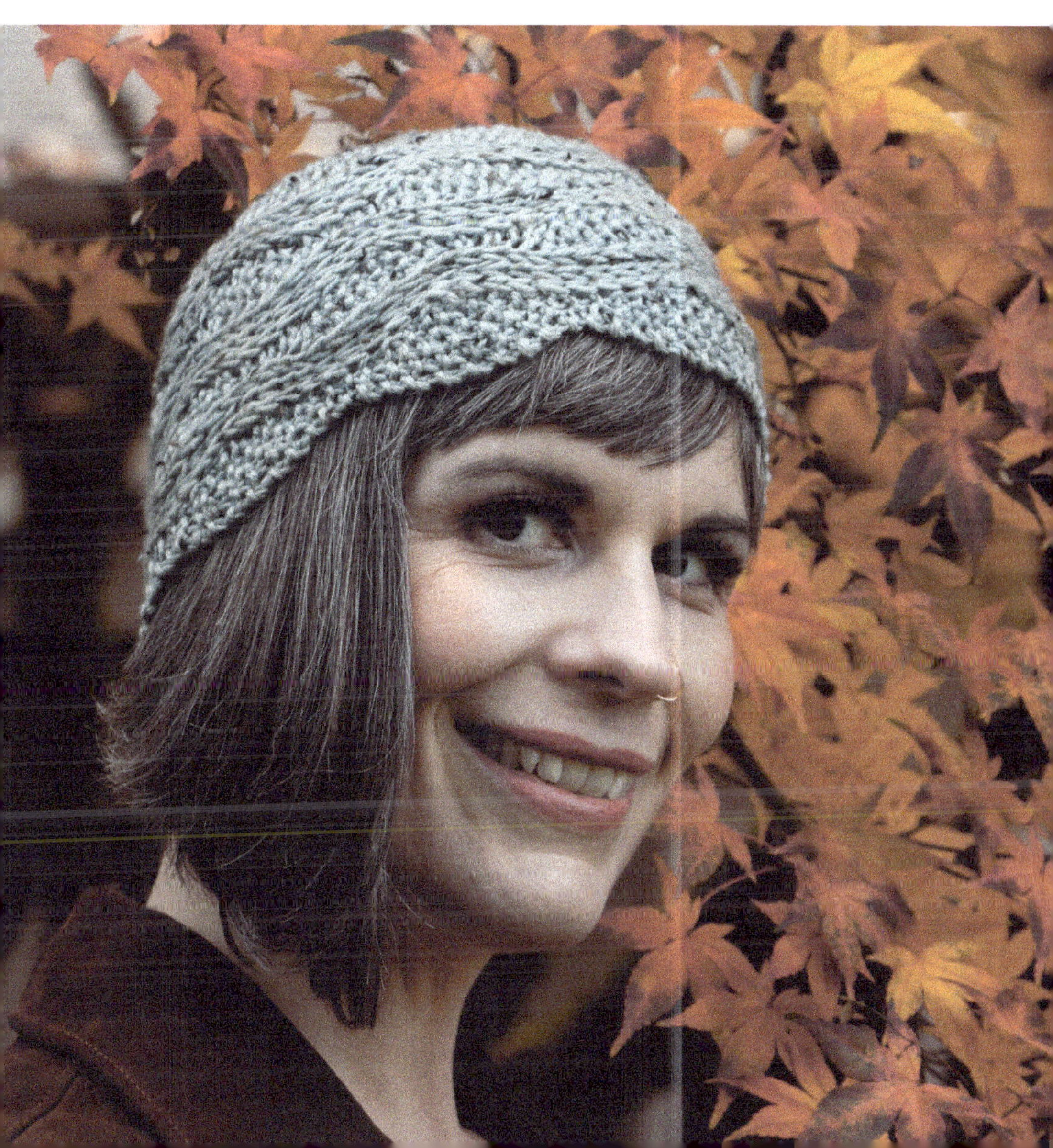

Row 4: P1, sl1, [k1, sl1] twice, p1, [k1, p1] twice, sl1, [k1, sl1] five times, [p1, k1] three times.

Row 5: [K1, p1] twice, k1, k2tog, [p1, k1] five times, m1, [p1, k1] twice, k2tog, [p1, k1] twice, m1, k1.

Row 6: P1, k1, [sl1, k1] three times, [p1, k1] twice, [sl1, k1]six times, [p1, k1] twice.

Row 7: [K1, p1] twice, k2tog, [p1, k1] five times, m1, [k1, p1] twice, k2tog, [p1, k1] twice, m1, k2.

Row 8: P1, k1, p1, [sl1, k1] twice, sl1, [p1, k1] twice, p1, [sl1, k1] five times, sl1, [p1, k1] twice.

Row 9: K1, p1, k1, k2tog, [p1, k1] twice, m1, [p1, k1] five times, k2tog, [p1, k1] twice, m1, p1, k2.

Row 10: [P1, k1] twice, [sl1, k1] three times, p1, k1, p1, [sl1, k1] twice, sl1, p1, [k1, sl1] three times, k1, p1, k1.

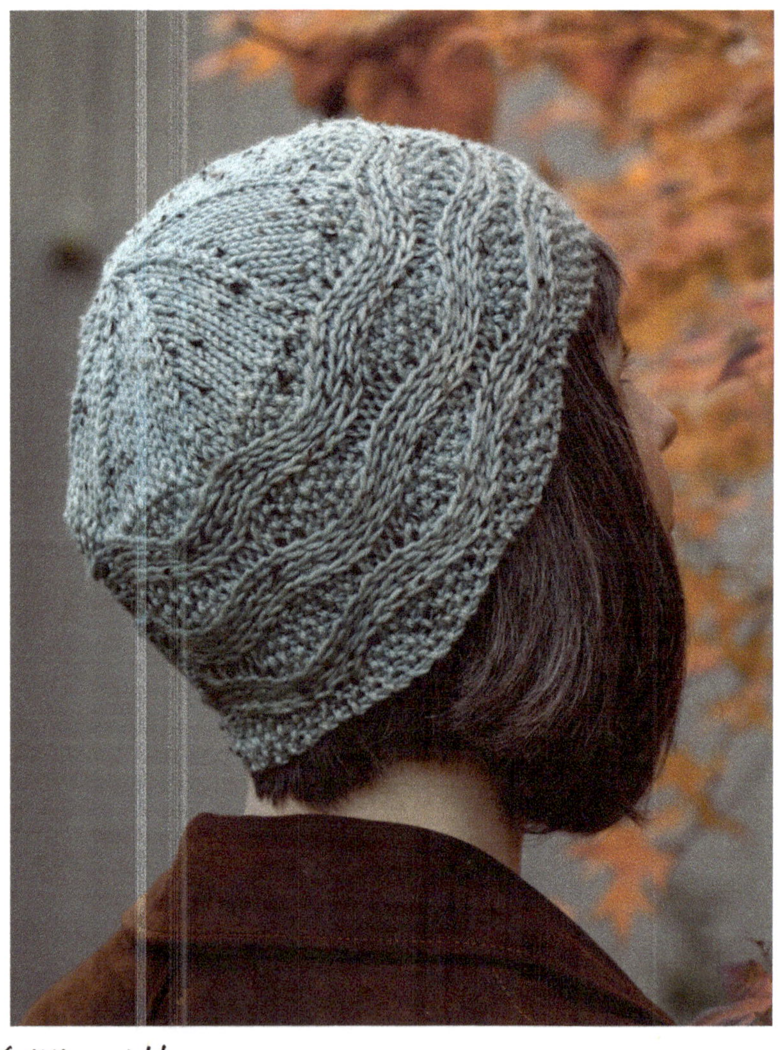

Waves Chart

Legend:
knit
RS: knit stitch
WS: purl stitch
purl
RS: purl stitch
WS: knit stitch
make one
M
ssk
k2tog
slip
WS: Slip stitch as if to purl,
holding yarn in front
V
Created in KnitVisualizer (www.knitfoundry.com)

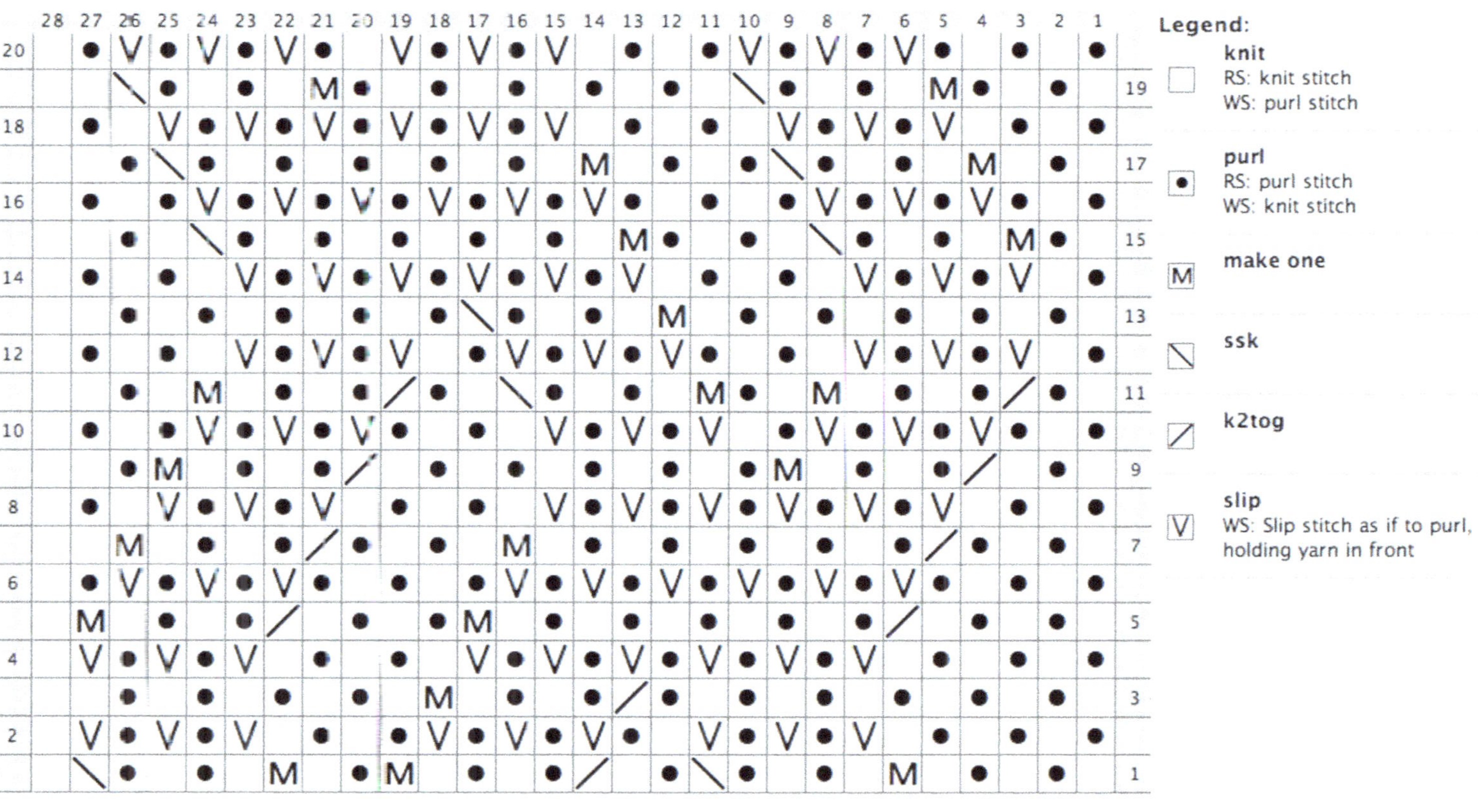

Row 11: K1, p1, k2tog, [p1, k1] twice, [m1, k1, p1] twice, k1, p1, ssk, k1, p1, k2tog, [p1, k1] twice, m1, k1, p1, k2.
Row 12: [P1, k1] twice, p1, [sl1, k1] twice, sl1, p1, [k1, sl1] three times, [k1, p1] twice, [sl1, k1] twice, sl1, p1, k1.
Row 13: [K1, p1] five times, k1, m1, [k1, p1] twice, ssk, [p1, k1] five times, k1.
Row 14: [P1, k1] twice, p1, [sl1, k1] five times, sl1, [p1, k1] twice, p1, [sl1, k1] twice, sl1, p1, k1.
Row 15: K1, p1, m1, [k1, p1] twice, ssk, [k1, p1] twice, m1, [k1, p1] five times, ssk, k1, p1, k2.
Row 16: [P1, k1] twice, [sl1, k1] six times, [p1, k1] twice, [sl1, k1] three times, p1, k1.
Row 17: K1, p1, k1, m1, [k1, p1] twice, ssk, [p1, k1] twice, m1, [k1, p1] five times, ssk, p1, k2.
Row 18: P1, k1, p1, [sl1, k1] five times, sl1, [p1, k1] twice, p1, [sl1, k1] twice, sl1, [p1, k1] twice.
Row 19: [K1, p1] twice, m1, [k1, p1] twice, ssk, [k1, p1] five times, m1, [k1, p1] twice, ssk, k2.
Row 20: P1, k1, [sl1, k1] three times, p1, [sl1, k1] twice, sl1, [p1, k1] twice, [sl1, k1] three times, [p1, k1] twice.

Repeat rows 1 - 20 (or the waves chart) seven [eight] more times (eight [nine] reps total).
BO all sts. (If you are grafting the work, do not bind off and leave the sts on the needle.)
Block flat.
Seam (or graft) the CO and BO edges together to form a tube.

Crown (worked in the round)
Starting at the seam and working from the right side, pick up and knit 80 [88] sts along the left selvedge edge of the band. Place a marker every 10 [11] sts.
Next rnd: Knit.
Decr Rnd: *Knit to 2 sts before the marker, k2tog, slm, rep from * to end of rnd. - 8 sts decreased
Knit two rnds.
Work one decr rnd followed by one knit rnd until only 8 sts remain.
Cut the yarn leaving a 6 - 8 inch / 15 - 20cm tail.
Using a tapestry needle, thread the yarn through the remaining sts slipping them off the needle. Cinch the yarn to close the top of the hat.
Weave in ends and block to shape.

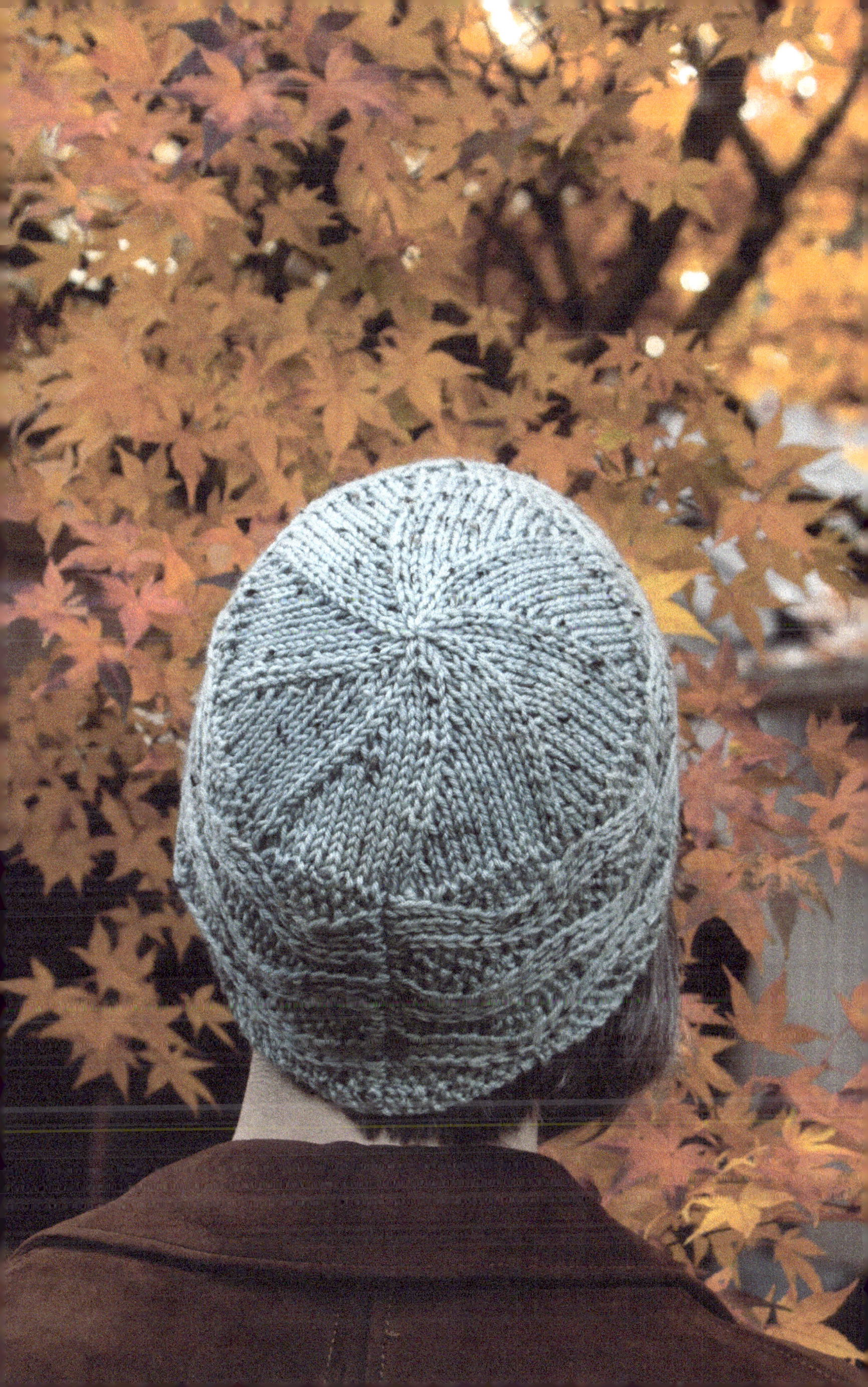

Ryberry Yarns

Hillsboro, OR

Kathy started knitting later in life, after taking a class at a big box store. But it wasn't until she discovered the Local Yarn Store, that her love of yarn was truly born. In 2016, she tried her hand at yarn dyeing. It started as a Christmas break project with her 10-year-old daughter, but quickly blossomed into a passion. When Kathy realized that she was producing more yarn than she could possibly knit, she did the logical thing and opened an etsy shop. In the early days, she was primarily dyeing one of a kind skeins in small lots, and sold enough to pay for the hobby.

Things really took off in 2017 when Kathy was contacted by Knit Crate to collaborate on subscription boxes. Kathy was now producing larger batches of repeatable colorways. After deliberating with her husband and daughter, she made the official decision to turn her hobby into a part time home business, and Ryberry Yarns was born. Since then Kathy has been slowly building her business both online and with local yarn stores.

Kathy is still dyeing yarn in small batches in her kitchen but her colors are repeatable and very much her own. She produces eye catching, highly saturated, and unusual colors that appeal to knitters looking for something just a little different.

In her day job Kathy is a Senior Buyer for a regional electronics manufacturing services company. It's a high-stress analytical job with a customer base that has included defense, aerospace, medical, and communications companies. Ryberry Yarns is Kathy's creative outlet and provides much needed stress relief.

Website: www.ryberryyarns.com
Instagram: @ryberry_yarns
Email: info@RyberryYarns.com

One thing that has really struck me about Kathy is her multi-layered life. She manages to find time to give to her yarn business, her family, and her day job. Each part is distinct but also interacts with the other parts of her life to create a beautiful whole. The mitts that I designed for her have an innovative two part, layered construction that creates a comfortable and unusual mitt.

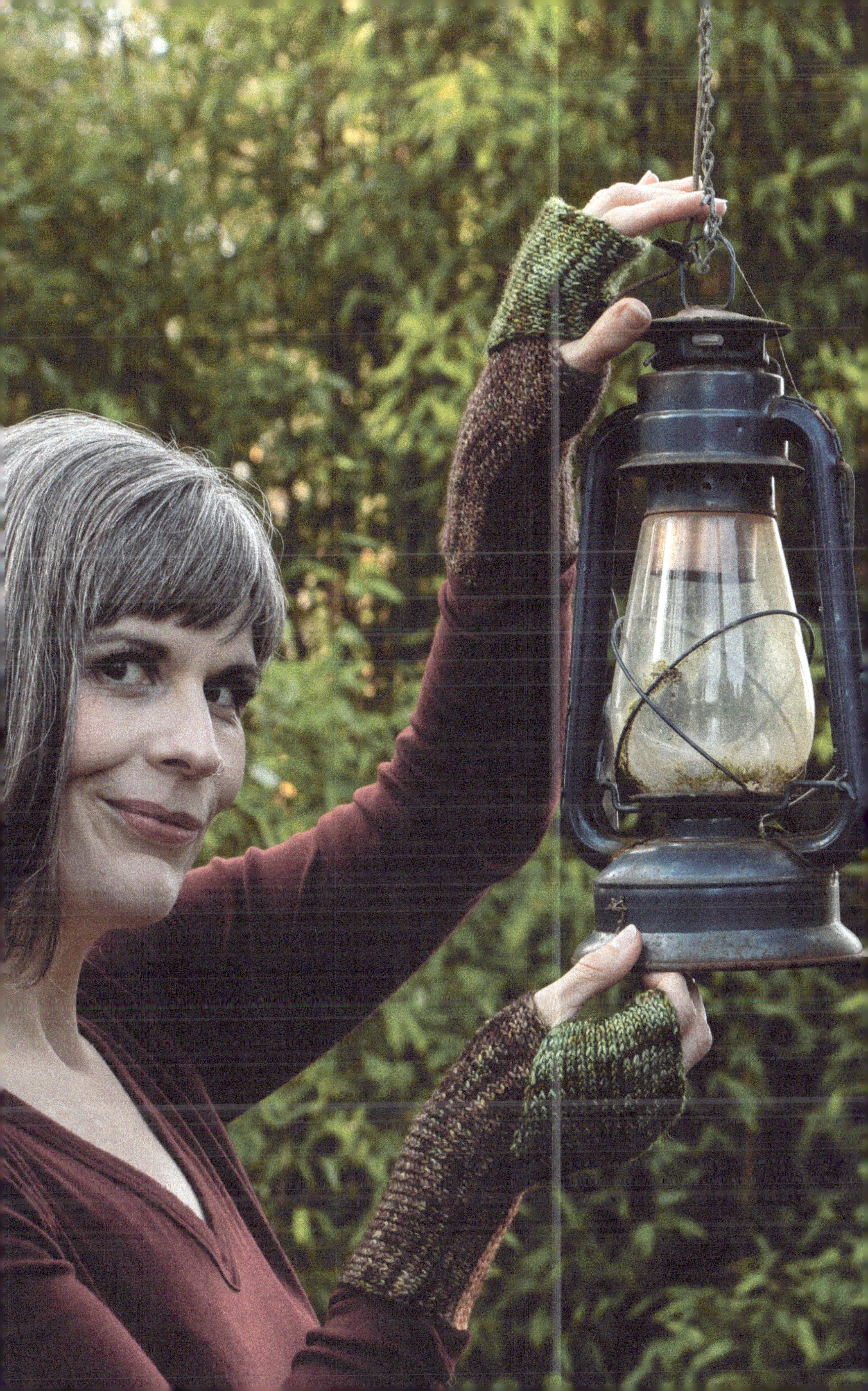

Layers

FINISHED MEASURMENTS
Hand Circumference: 7 inches / 18cm (with some stretch)
Length: 7 inches / 18cm

YARN
Fingering weight yarn:
Hand color: 85 yards / 77m
Arm color: 150 yards / 137m
Join color: 25 yards / 23m

Yarn provided by Ryberry Yarns
Mini-Skeins!: 85% superwash merino, 15% nylon
87 yards per 20g
Colorways: Tobacco Road (hand), Lauma's Tree (arm), and Red Fox (join)

OTHER MATERIALS
Two US size 4 (3.5mm) 36 inch / 90cm circular needles (the second needle can be any length) or size needed to obtain gauge

Scrap yarn or stitch holders

Tapestry needle

GAUGE
40 sts = 4 inches / 10cm in twisted rib (unblocked and unstretched)
CO an even number of sts.
Row 1 (RS): *k1tbl, p1, rep from * to end of row.
Row 2 (WS): *K1, p1, rep from * to end of row.

PATTERN NOTE
The pattern is written assuming that you are familiar with a continuous cast on method such as Judy's Magic Cast On. A video tutorial by Judy Becker can be found here: www.youtube.com/watch?v=1pmxRDZ-cwo

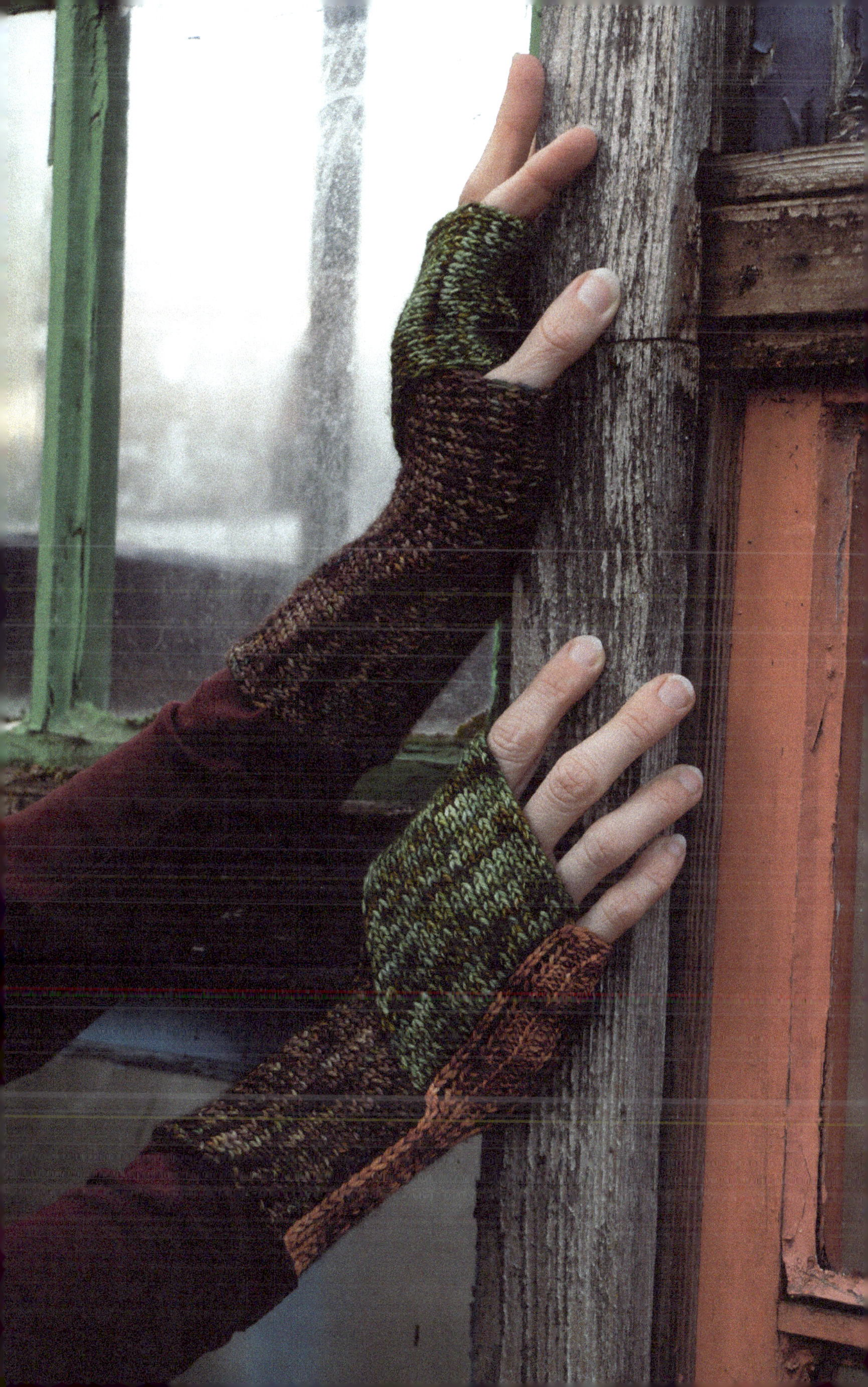

PATTERN

Hand (Make 2 using the hand color)

With both ends of one 36 inch / 90cm circular needle CO 80 sts using the continuous cast on (40 sts/needle tip).

Work the following with one set of 40 sts. (Slide the other 40 sts onto the cable portion of the needle.)

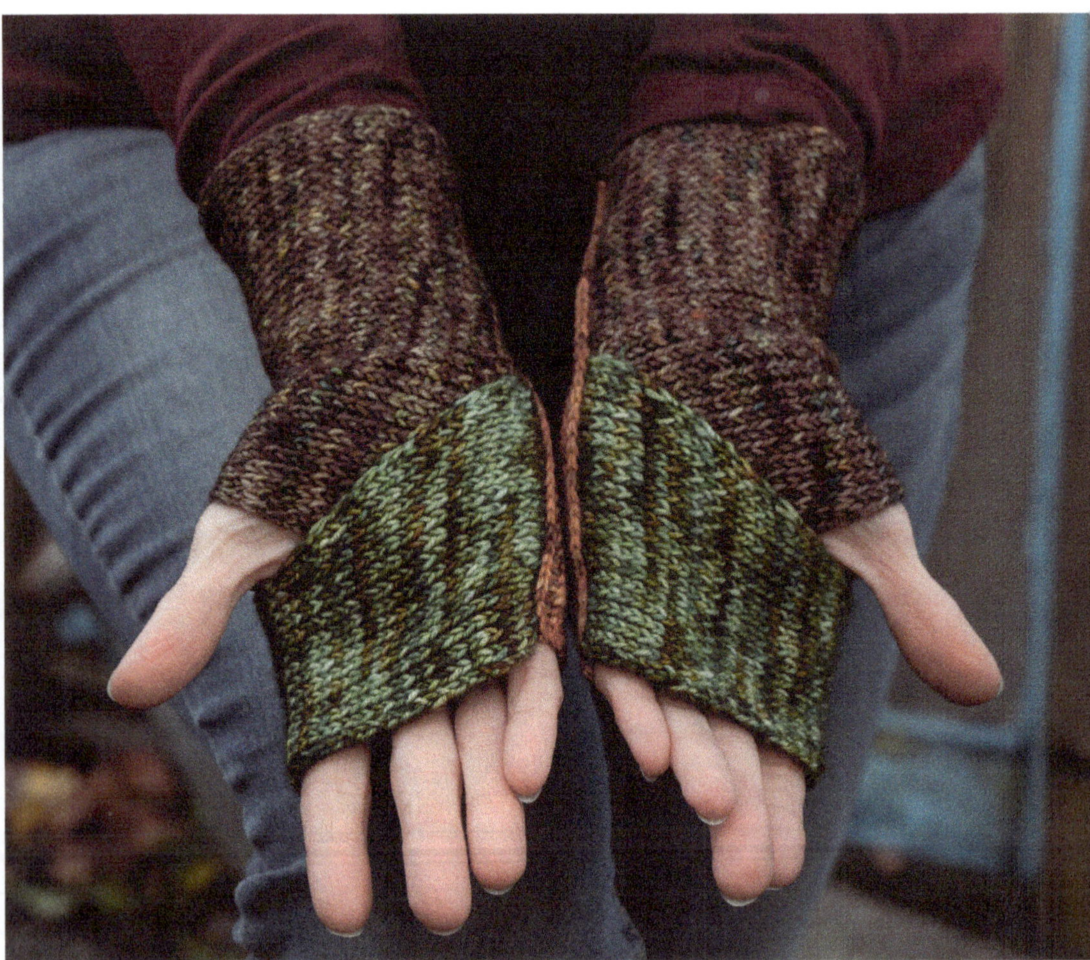

Row 1 (RS): K1, k1, p1, *k1tbl, p1, rep from * to last st, p1.
Row 2 (WS): K1, *k1, p1, rep from * to the last st, p1.
Row 3: K1, ssk, *k1tbl, p1, rep from * to last st, p1.
Row 4: K1, *k1, p1, rep from * to last 2 sts, p2.
Row 5: K1, ssk, p1, *k1tbl, p1, rep from * to last st, p1.
Row 6: K1, *k1, p1, rep from * to last st, p1.
Rep rows 3 - 6 five more times (six reps total). You will now have 28 sts.

Row 7: K2, m1, p1, *k1tbl, p1, rep from * to last st, p1.
Row 8: K1, *k1, p1, rep from * to last 2 sts, p2.
Row 9: K2, m1, *k1tbl, p1, rep from * to last st, p1.
Row 10: K1, *k1, p1, rep from * to last st, p1.
Rep rows 7 - 10 five more times (six reps total). You will now have 40 sts.
Rep rows 1 and 2 once more.
Cut the yarn leaving a 6 - 8 inch / 15 - 20cm tail. and put both sets of sts on holders or scrap yarn.

Arm (Make 2 using the arm color)
With both ends of one 36 inch / 90cm circular needle CO 144 sts using the continuous cast on (72 sts/needle tip).
Work the following with one set of 72 sts. (Slide the other 72 sts onto the cable portion of the needle.)

Row 1 (RS): K1, k1, p1, *k1tbl, p1, rep from * to last st, p1.
Row 2 (WS): K1, *k1, p1, rep from * to the last st, p1.
Row 3: K1, ssk, *k1tbl, p1, rep from * to last st, p1.
Row 4: K1, *k1, p1, rep from * to last 2 sts, p2.
Row 5: K1, ssk, p1, *k1tbl, p1, rep from * to last st, p1.
Row 6: K1, *k1, p1, rep from * to last st, p1.
Rep rows 3 - 6 five more times (six reps total). You will now have 60 sts.
Row 7: K2, m1, p1, *k1tbl, p1, rep from * to last st, p1.
Row 8: K1, *k1, p1, rep from * to last 2 sts, p2.
Row 9: K2, m1, *k1tbl, p1, rep from * to last st, p1.
Row 10: K1, *k1, p1, rep from * to last st, p1.
Rep rows 7 - 10 five more times (six reps total). You will now have 72 sts.
Rep rows 1 and 2 once more.
Cut the yarn leaving a 6 - 8 inch / 15 - 20cm tail and leave the sts on the needle.

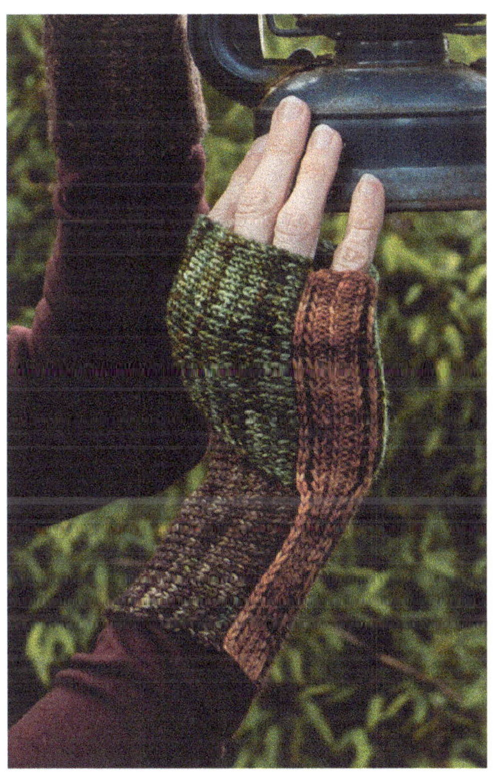

Joining

See photo 1 for proper orientation of the pieces and location of "the first st" for each piece.

Using the second needle, slip the first st from the right edge of the hand then the first st from the right edge of the arm onto the new needle. These will be called paired sts. Be sure that you are working from the right side on both pieces and that they are oriented so that the hand is layered on top of the arm. Continue slipping one st from the hand and one st from the arm until all the hand sts have been transferred. You will now have 40 paired sts. Slip the remaining 32 arm sts onto the needle.

PHOTO 1

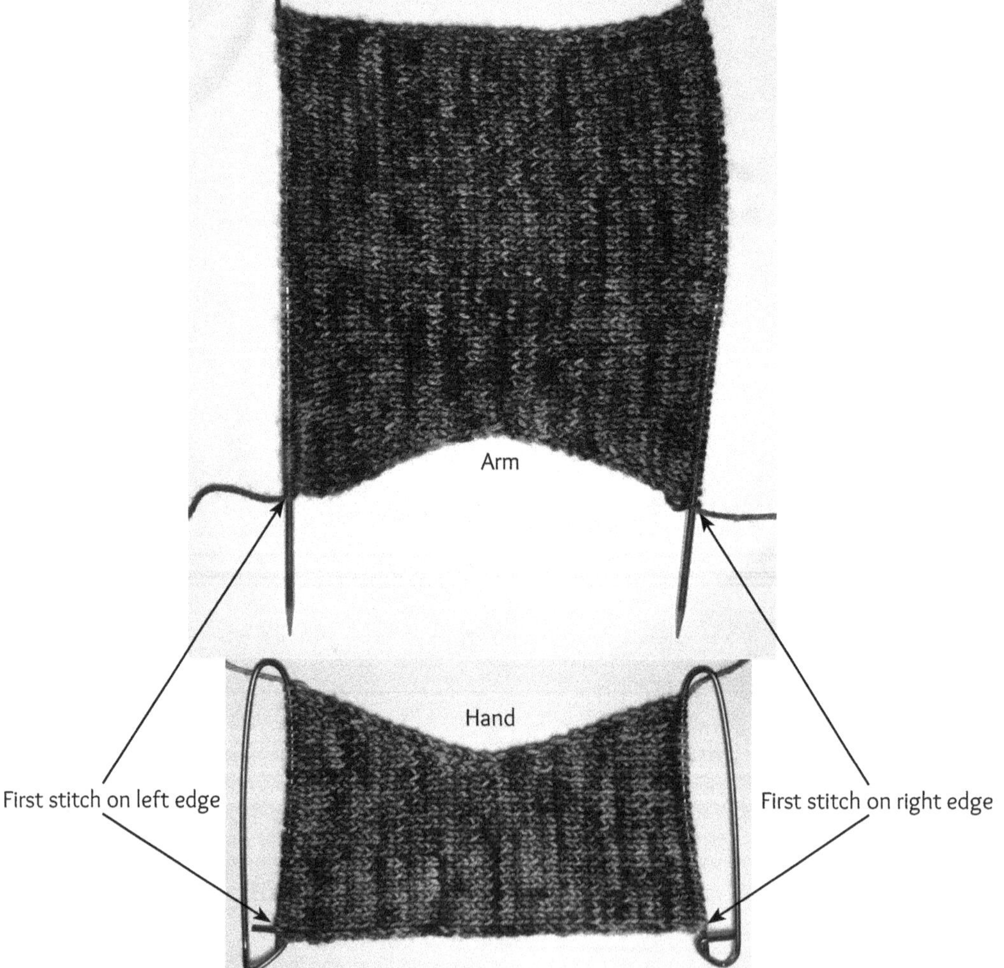

Repeat this process for the left edges using the RH tip of the first needle. See photo 2 for correct set up.

The mitts are joined by knitting a narrow strip from the bottom to the top, connecting live stitches from the mitts at the beginning and end of each row. This process is similar to a knitted on border.

With the join color, CO 7 sts onto the LH needle tip. See photo 2.
Row 1 (RS): Sl1wyib, [k1tbl, p1] twice, k1tbl, sssk.
Row 2 (WS): Sl1wyif, [p1, k1] twice, p1, p3tog.
Rep rows 1 and 2 until you've worked all 32 unpaired arm sts.
When you reach the paired sts, continue as before treating each pair of sts as one st.
When all of the arm and hand sts have been worked, BO the remaining 7 sts.
Weave in ends.
Mitts are shown here unblocked. If you choose to block yours, take care to preserve the three dimensional character of the fabric.

Photo 2

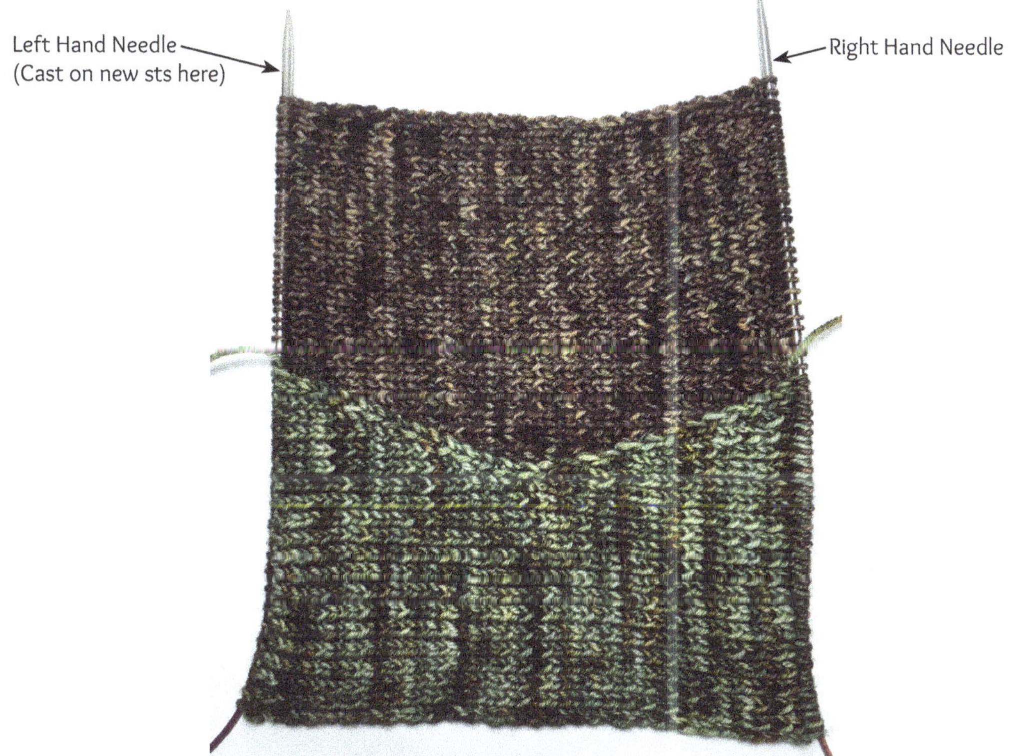

Driftwood Farms

Lakeside, OR

Driftwood Farms Yarn and Candle is a mother-daughter team located on the southern Oregon coast. Mom Kimberly is the yarn dyer of the pair while daughter Jessica dyes fiber and makes candles. Kimberly got started dying yarn when she couldn't find fun colors to knit things for her grandkids. She decided to try dyeing her own yarn and it took off. After getting her hands in all of that natural fiber, she was hooked and never looked back.

Kimberly dyes yarn in her home kitchen in the mornings and draws inspiration from the outdoors. She cherishes her big family. They are the most important part of her life and bring her peace and keep her grounded.

Shop: www.etsy.com/shop/DriftwoodFarmsYarnCo
Instagram: @driftwoodfarmsyarnandcandleco
Facebook: Driftwood Farms Yarn & Candle
Email: driftwoodfarmsyarnandcandle@outlook.com

I asked Kimberly about where she lived and as part of her description she wrote, "I can hear the ocean from my backyard and after a storm when everything is quiet, the surf is so loud. I love the smell of the sea." The shawl I designed for her was inspired by this beautiful image she painted for me of the sound and the smell of the surf after a storm.

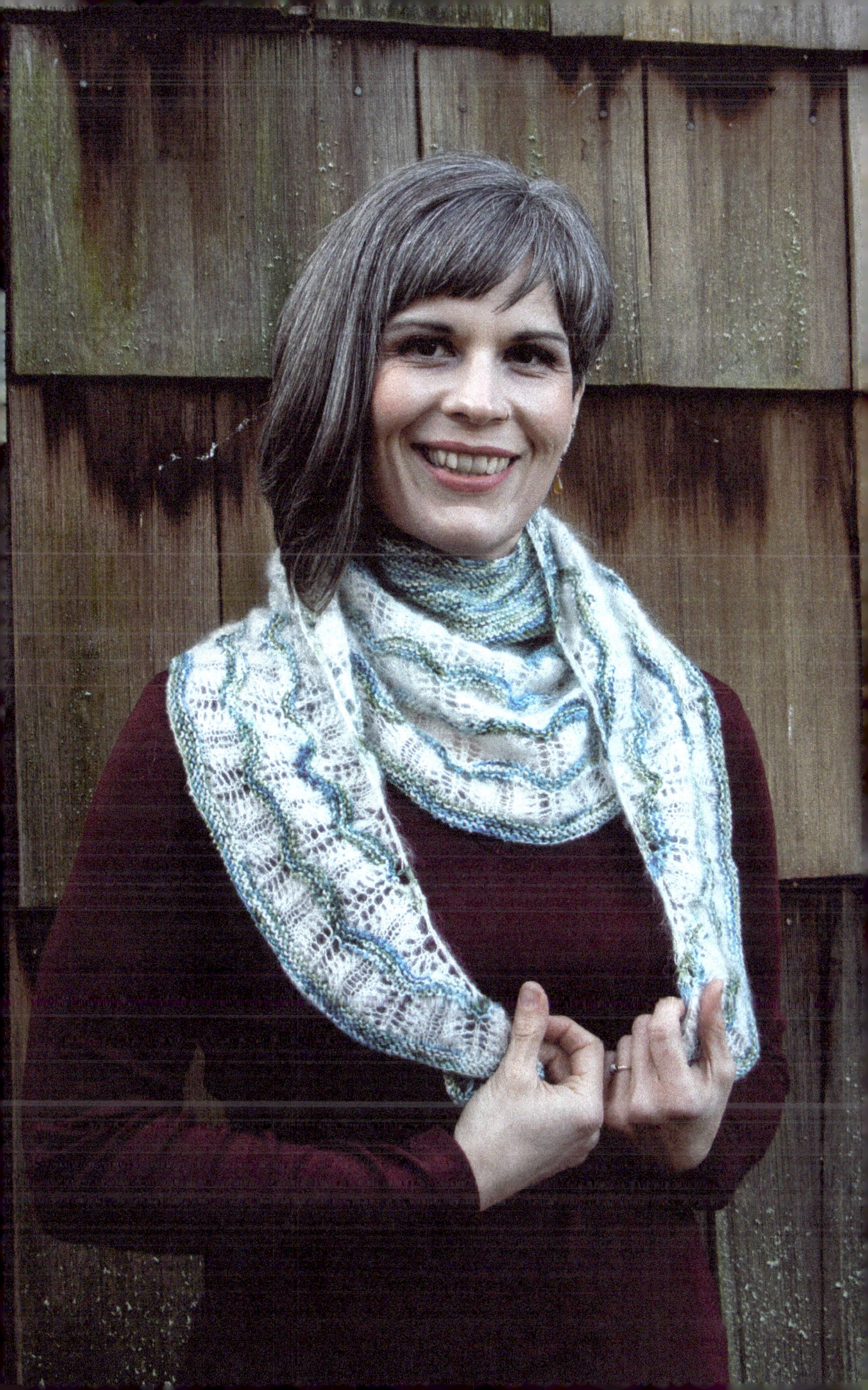

Scent of the Sea

FINISHED MEASUREMENTS
Wingspan: 67 inches / 170cm
Depth: 13 inches / 33cm

YARN
325 yards / 297m of fingering weight yarn
250 yards / 228m of lace weight yarn

Yarn provided by Driftwood Farms
Osprey Fingering: 100% New Zealand SW polwarth
437 yards / 400m per 100g
Colorway: Stormy Monday
Breezy Mohair: 72% superkid mohair, 28% mulberry silk
459 yards / 420m per 50g
Colorway: Snowfall

OTHER MATERIALS
US size 4 (3.5mm) 30 inch / 75cm or longer circular needle or size
needed to obtain gauge

Tapestry needle

GAUGE
24 sts = 4 inches / 10cm in garter stitch

SPECIAL STITCHES
Knit, yarn over, knit (kyok): Knit, then yo, then knit again into the same
stitch. Three sts made from 1 st.

PATTERN NOTES
When you are working a section with one yarn, carry the second yarn
neatly along the selvedge edge by twisting the two yarns around each
other before starting each RS row.

Each time you switch yarns, be sure to leave plenty of slack so you do
not constrict the top edge of the shawl. One easy way to do this is to
add a yo to the start of the row and drop it at the end of the next row.

PATTERN
Set Up
With fingering weight yarn CO 9 sts.
Rows 1 and 2: Knit.
Row 3 (RS): K2, yo, knit to last 2 sts, yo, k2.
Row 4 (WS): K2, kyok, knit to last 3 sts, kyok, k2.
Rep rows 3 and 4 until there are 62 yos along the top edge (195 sts)

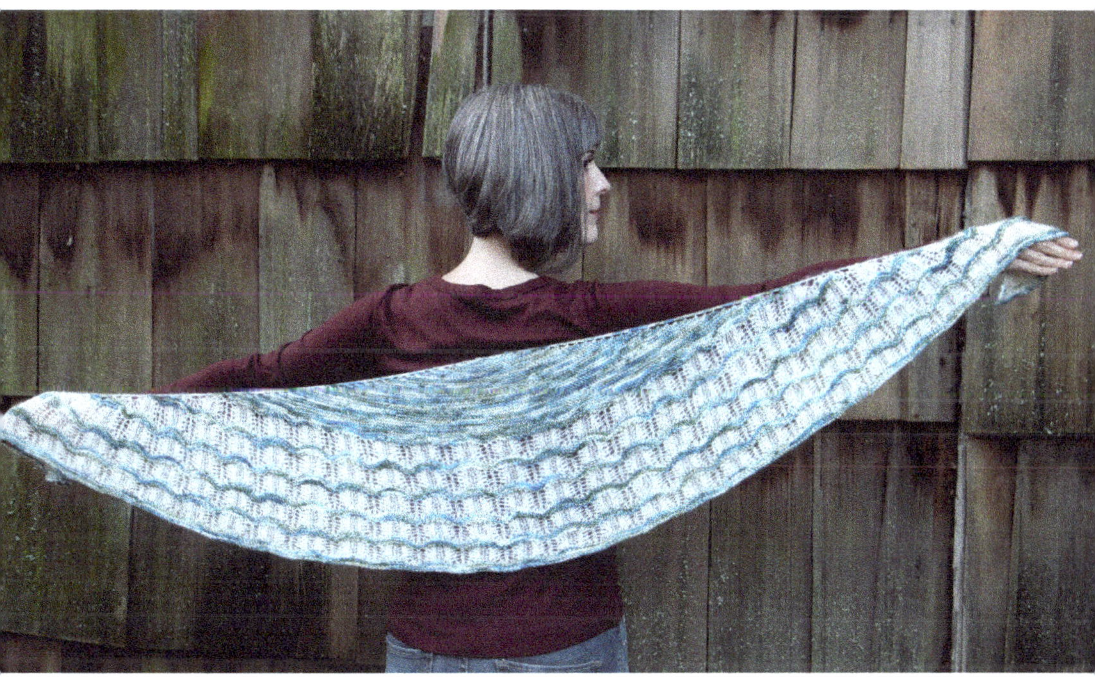

Main Body Section
Switch to lace weight yarn.
Row 5: K2, yo, k2tog, k2tog, yo, [k1, yo] three times, ssk, ssk, *k1,
k2tog, k2tog, yo, [k1, yo] three times, ssk, ssk, rep from * to last 2 sts,
yo, k2.
Row 6: K2, kyok, purl to last 3 sts, kyok, k2.
Row 7: K2, yo, k2, *k1, k2tog, k2tog, yo, [k1, yo] three times, ssk, ssk,
rep from * to last 5 sts, k3, yo, k2.
Row 8: K2, kyok, purl to last 3 sts, kyok, k2.
Row 9: K2, yo, k5, *k1, k2tog, k2tog, yo, [k1, yo] three times, ssk, ssk,
rep from * to last 8 sts, k6, yo, k2.
Row 10: K2, kyok, purl to last 3 sts, kyok, k2.
Row 11: K2, yo, k3, yo, k1, yo, ssk, ssk, *k1, k2tog, k2tog, yo, [k1, yo]
three times, ssk, ssk, rep from * to last 11 sts, k1, k2tog, k2tog, yo, k1,
yo, k3, yo, k2.

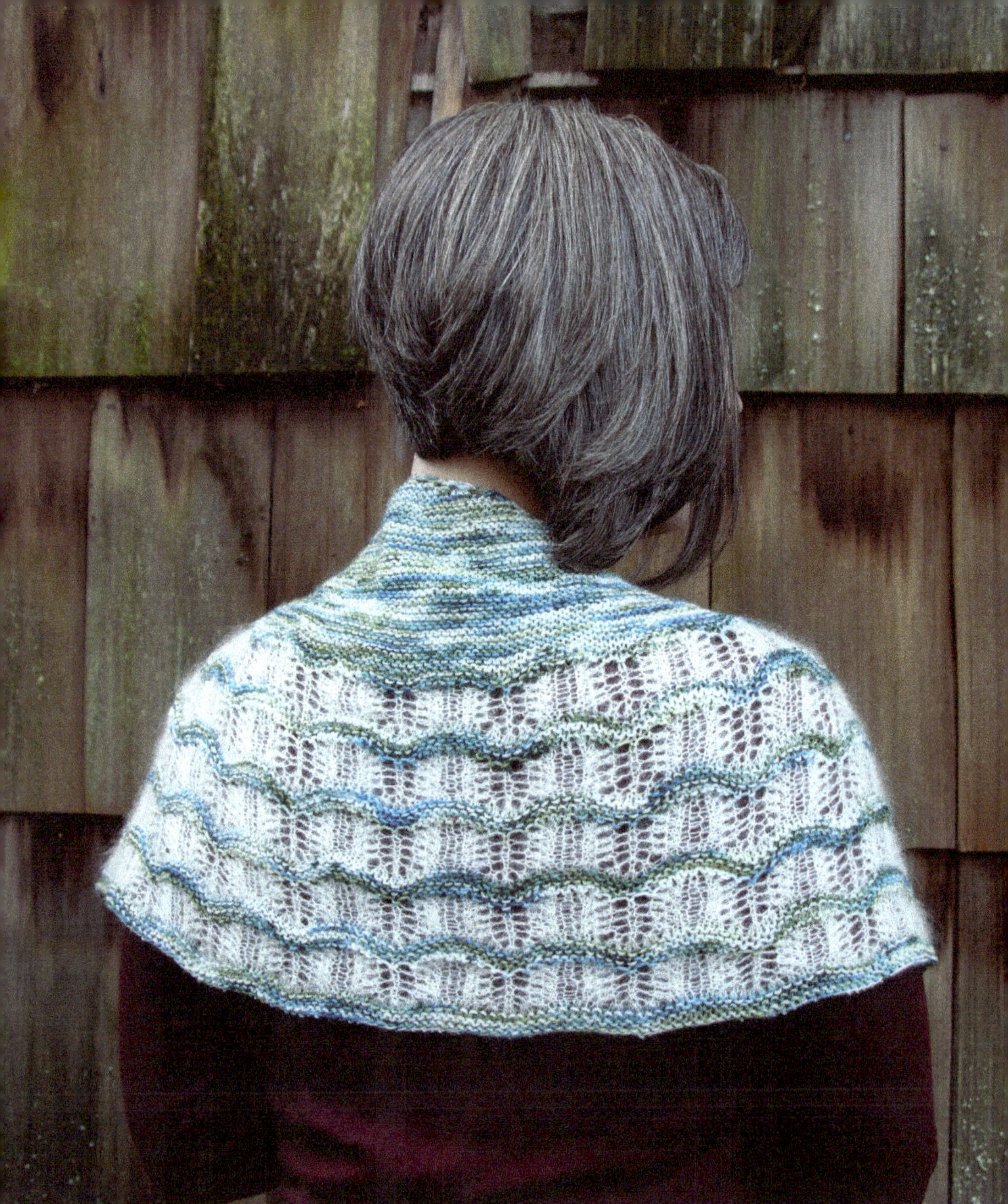

Row 12: K2, kyok, purl to last 3 sts, kyok, k2.
Row 13: K2, yo, k2tog, k2tog, yo, [k1, yo] three times, ssk, ssk, *k1, k2tog, k2tog, yo, [k1, yo] three times, ssk, ssk, rep from * to last 2 sts, yo, k2.
Row 14: K2, kyok, purl to last 3 sts, kyok, k2.
Switch to fingering weight yarn.
Row 15: K2, yo, knit to last 2 sts, yo, k2.
Row 16: K2, kyok, knit to last 3 sts, kyok, k2.
Rep rows 15 and 16 two more times (three reps total).

Rep the main body section until the shawl is the desired size ending after the third rep of row 16. (Shown with 5 reps of the main body section.)

With fingering weight yarn BO all sts as follows:
K2, insert the tip of the LH needle into the front of the 2 sts on the RH needle, knit the 2 together through the back loops, *k1, insert the tip of the LH needle into the front of the 2 sts on the RH needle, knit the 2 together through the back loops, rep from * until all sts are bound off.

Weave in ends and block to shape.

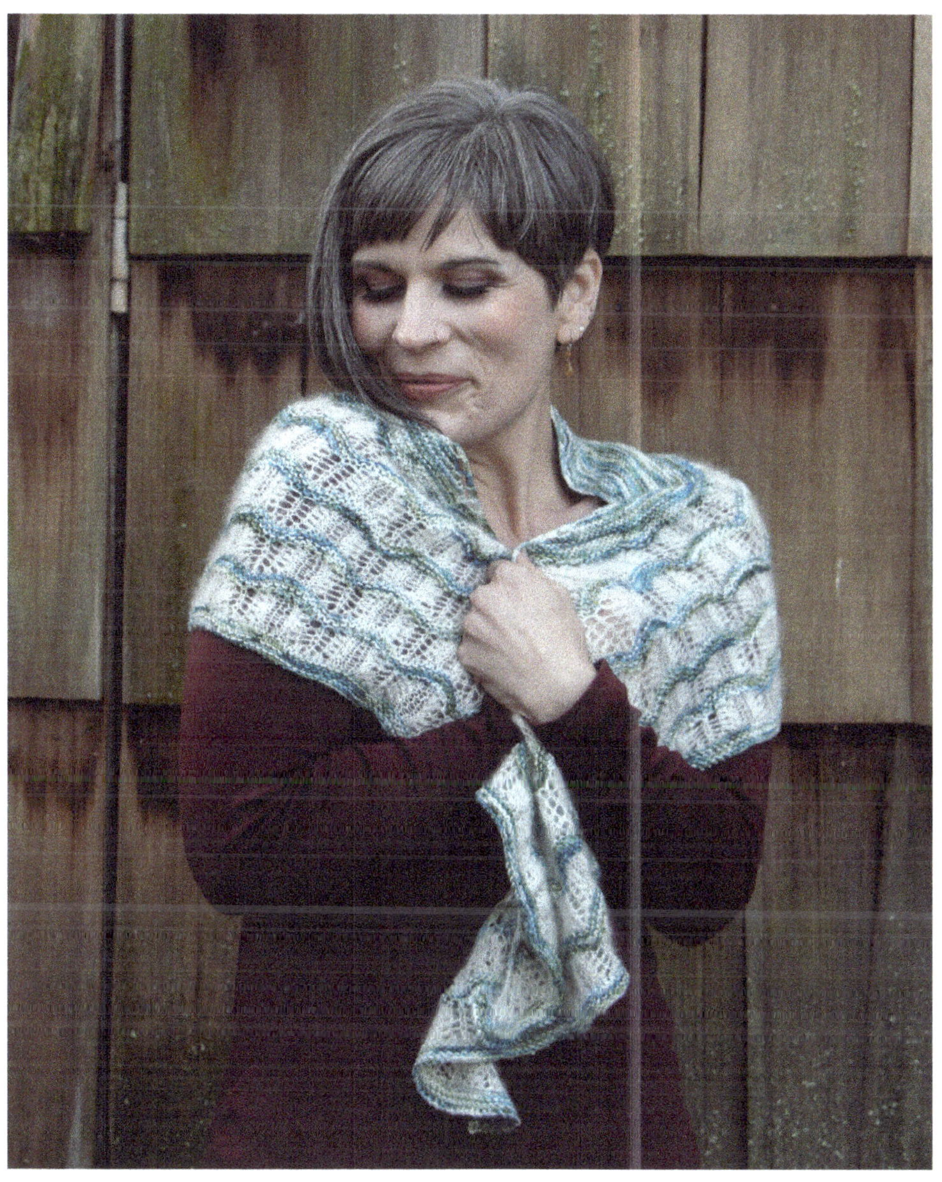

Wee Chickadee Wool Co.

Medford, OR

Hey Chickadee! Jennifer McDaniel is the creator behind Wee Chickadee
Wool Co. She is an avid knitter, spinner, weaver, felter, and dyer and
loves all aspects of working with wool as a medium for self-expression
and creativity. The fiber arts provide endless possibilities and a feeling
of self-reliance. Honestly, no one is going to go cold or naked with her
around when the Zombie apocalypse happens!

Jennifer started Wee Chickadee with her sister Christina in 2013 after
attending Sock Summit in Portland, OR and falling in love with hand
dyed yarn. At that time hand dyed yarns were much harder to come by,
so they learned to dye for themselves. That love and passion evolved
into a desire to share their creations with others, and Wee Chickadee
was born. Christina has now moved on to become a full-time rockstar
Librarian. Jennifer continues to create and share her hand dyed yarn and
fiber with other fiber enthusiasts.

Besides creating with wool, Jennifer loves hiking and backpacking,
and can frequently be found out exploring the many trails around her
in Oregon. She took a small hiatus from the shop in 2019 to hike the
Pacific Crest Trail. She is currently working toward her certification to
become an Oregon Master Naturalist.

Jennifer loves nature as much as she loves working with wool, and the
two are definitely not mutually exclusive. She recently began learning
how to dye with plants and flowers. Using natural dyes is a fascinating
way to dye fiber and gives her a whole new appreciation for both the
plants used and the art of dyeing as a whole. Nature has always inspired
the colors she uses in her work and many of her colorways are a direct
reflection of the beauty of the natural world around her.

Shop: www.etsy.com/shop/WeeChickadeeWoolCo
Instagram: @wee.chickadee
Facebook: Wee Chickadee Wool Co.
Email: weechickadeewoolco@gmail.com

I found a kindred spirit with Jennifer. As we compared notes we quickly discovered that we shared a love of the wild open spaces that Oregon has to offer and regularly draw inspiration from the natural world around us. The pattern I settled on was inspired by Steen's Mountain in SE Oregon, which Jennifer describes as her "absolute favorite place in the world." She even cooked up a colorway just for this project that beautifully captures the soft, delicate tones of SE Oregon.

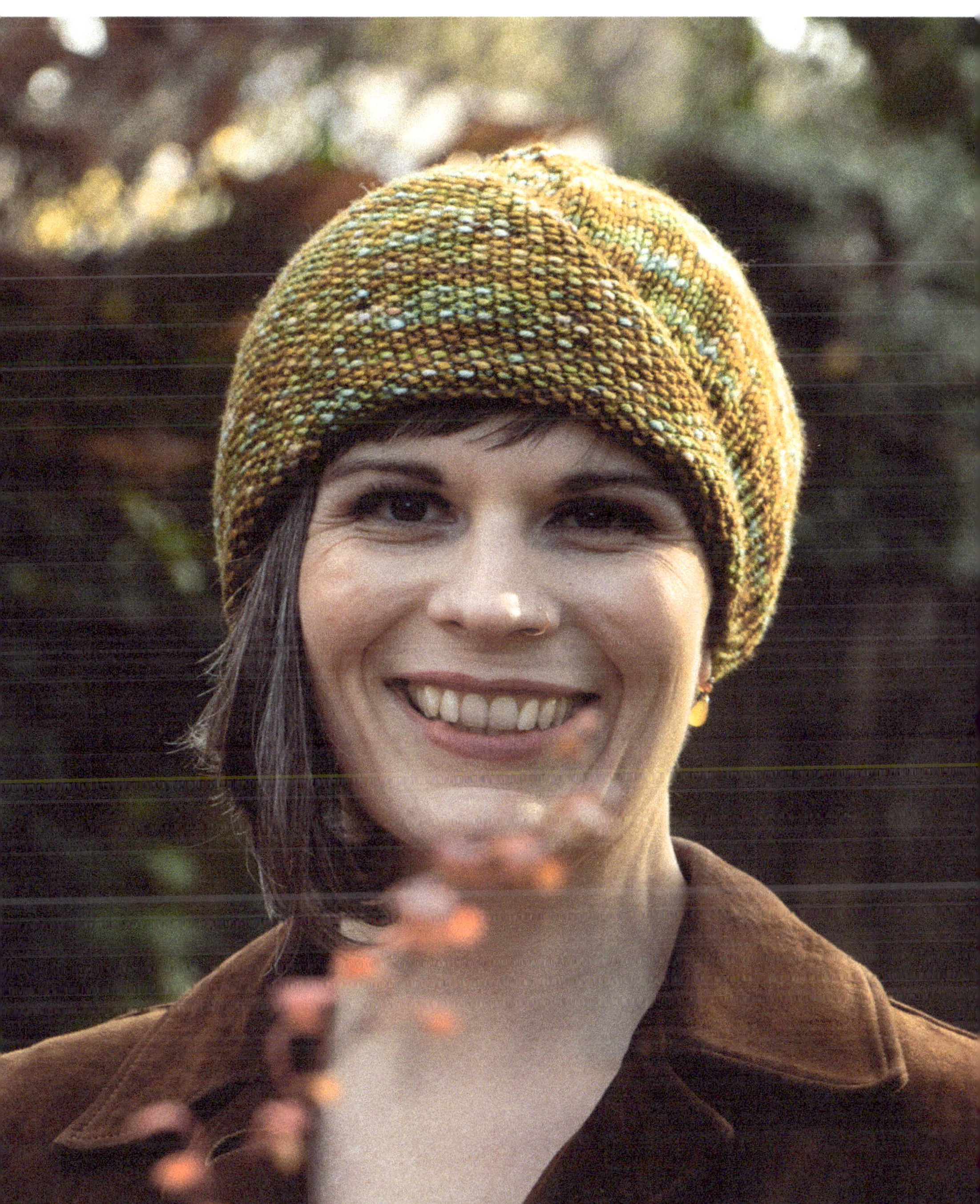

Steen's Mountain

Finished Measurments

Circumference: 17 inches / 43cm (Has plenty of stretch for larger heads.)
Height: 9 inches / 23cm

Yarn

225 yards / 205m of DK weight yarn

Yarn provided by Wee Chickadee
100% superwash merino DK
231 yards per 100g
Colorway: How Wild it Was

Other Materials

US size 6 (4mm) needles (you will need this size for knitting flat and knitting in the round) or size needed to obtain gauge
US size 9 (5.5mm) needles (used for knitting in the round)

8 stitch markers

Stitch holder

Tapestry needle

Gauge

20 sts = 4 inches / 10cm in k1, p1 ribbing on smaller needles

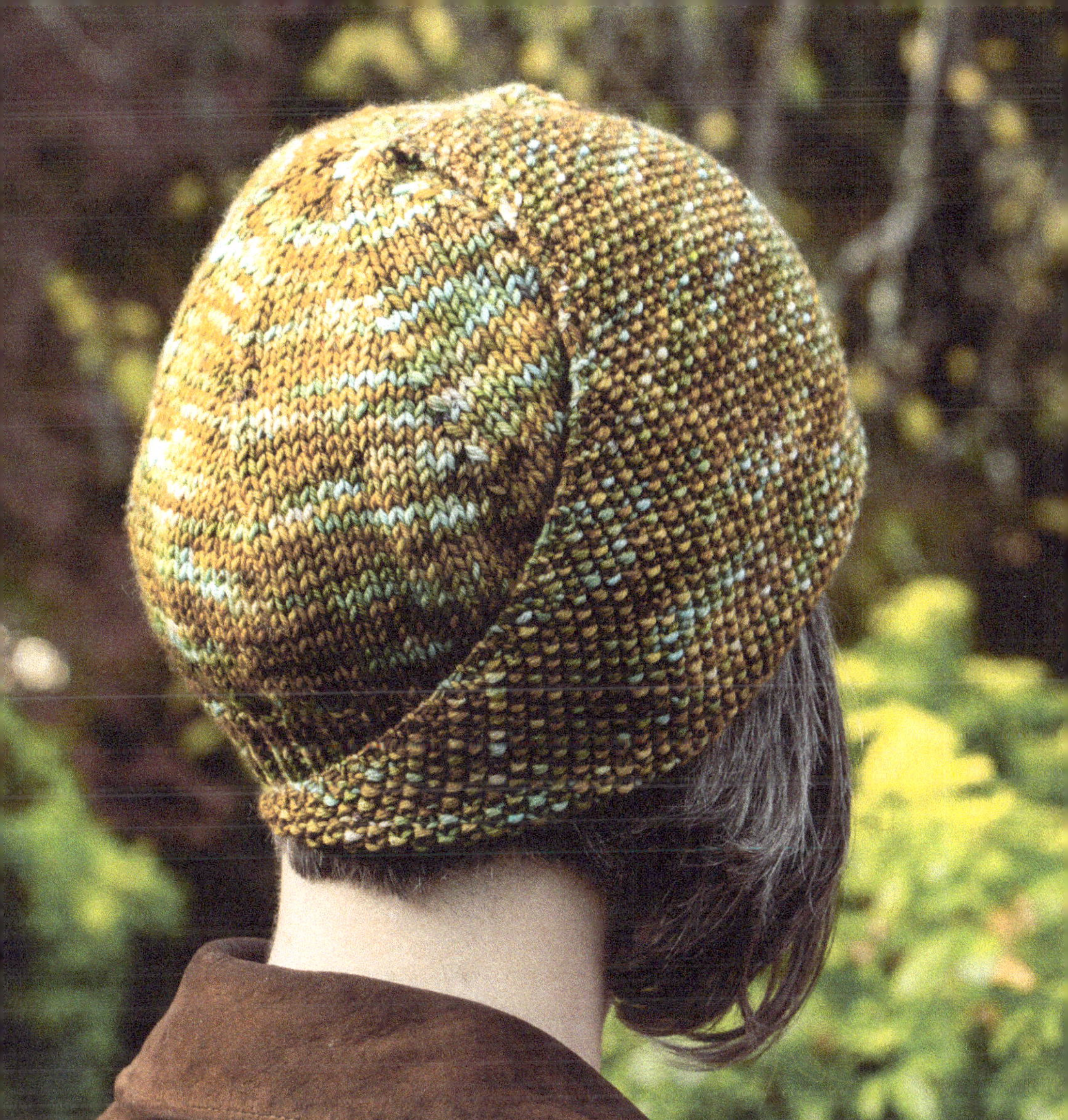

Pattern

Brim (worked flat)
With smaller needles CO 3 sts.
Row 1: K1, kfb, k1.
Row 2: K1, m1, k1, p1, m1, k1.
Row 3: K1, k1, p1, k1, p1, k1.
Row 4: K1, m1, *p1, k1, rep from * to last st, m1, k1.
Row 5: K1, *p1, k1, rep from * to last st, k1.
Row 6: K1, m1, *k1, p1, rep from * to last st, m1, k1.
Row 7: K1, *k1, p1, rep from * to last st, k1.
Rep rows 4 - 7 until you have 82 sts.
Leave the sts on the needle and block flat forming a triangle.

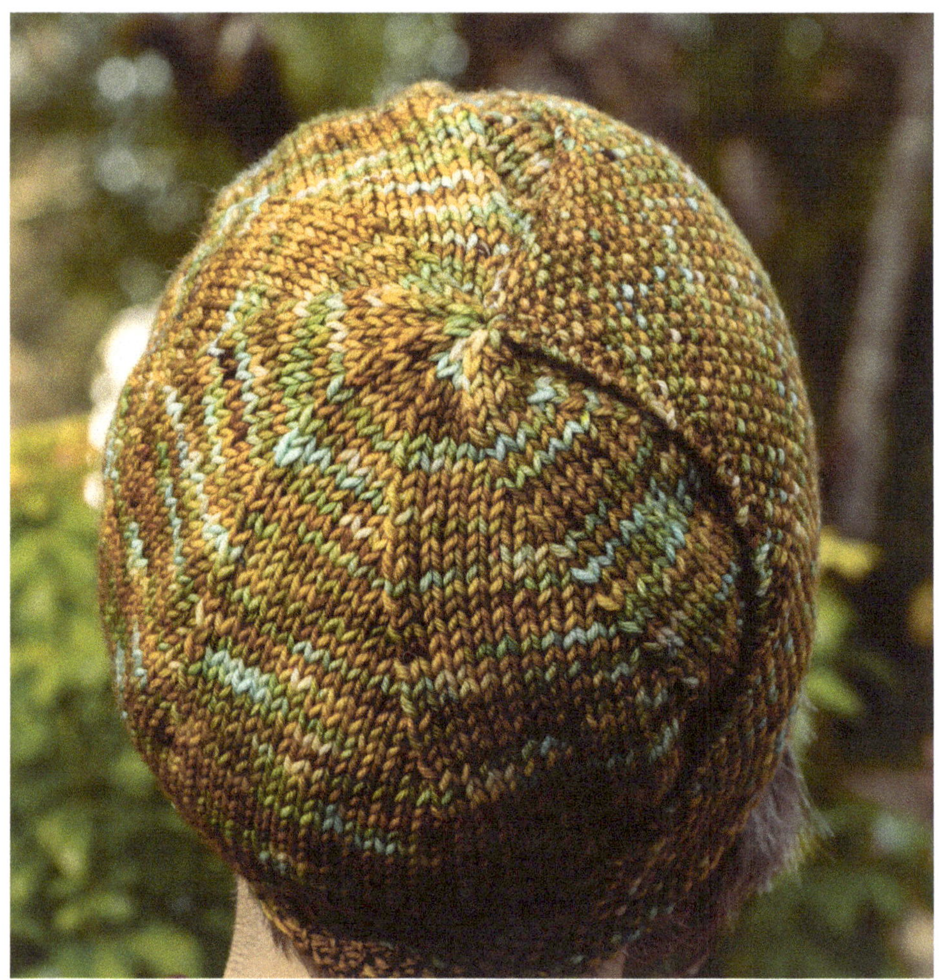

Crown (worked in the round)
CO 14 sts to the end of the last row worked above, then join the work in the round placing a marker to indicate the end of the rnd.
Work 2 inches in k1, p1 ribbing.
Switch to larger needles.
Incr Rnd: *K4, m1, rep from * to end of rnd. - 120 sts
Work 2 inches / 5cm even in stockinette stitch (knit all rnds). In the last rnd, place a marker every 15th stitch. Seven additional markers placed.

Crown Shaping
Rnd 1: *Ssk, knit to marker, sm, rep from * to end of rnd. - 8 sts decreased.
Rnds 2 and 3: Knit.
Rnd 4: *Ssk, knit to marker, sm, rep from * to end of rnd. - 8 sts decreased.

Rnd 5: Knit.
Rep rnds 4 and 5 until there are only 8 sts left.
Place the remaining sts on a holder and cut the yarn leaving a 6 - 8 inch /
15 - 20cm tail.
Block the crown to shape.
Join the tip of the brim to the top of the hat as follows:
Using the tail left from the crown on tapestry needle, slip through the
first 2 sts of the crown dropping them off the holder.
Stitch through the cast on edge of the point of the brim once.
Slip through the next crown st.
Stitch through the cast on edge of the point of the brim once.
Slip through the next crown st.
Stitch through the cast on edge of the point of the brim once.
Slip through the remaining crown sts.
Cinch the yarn to close the top of the hat.
Weave in ends and block to shape.

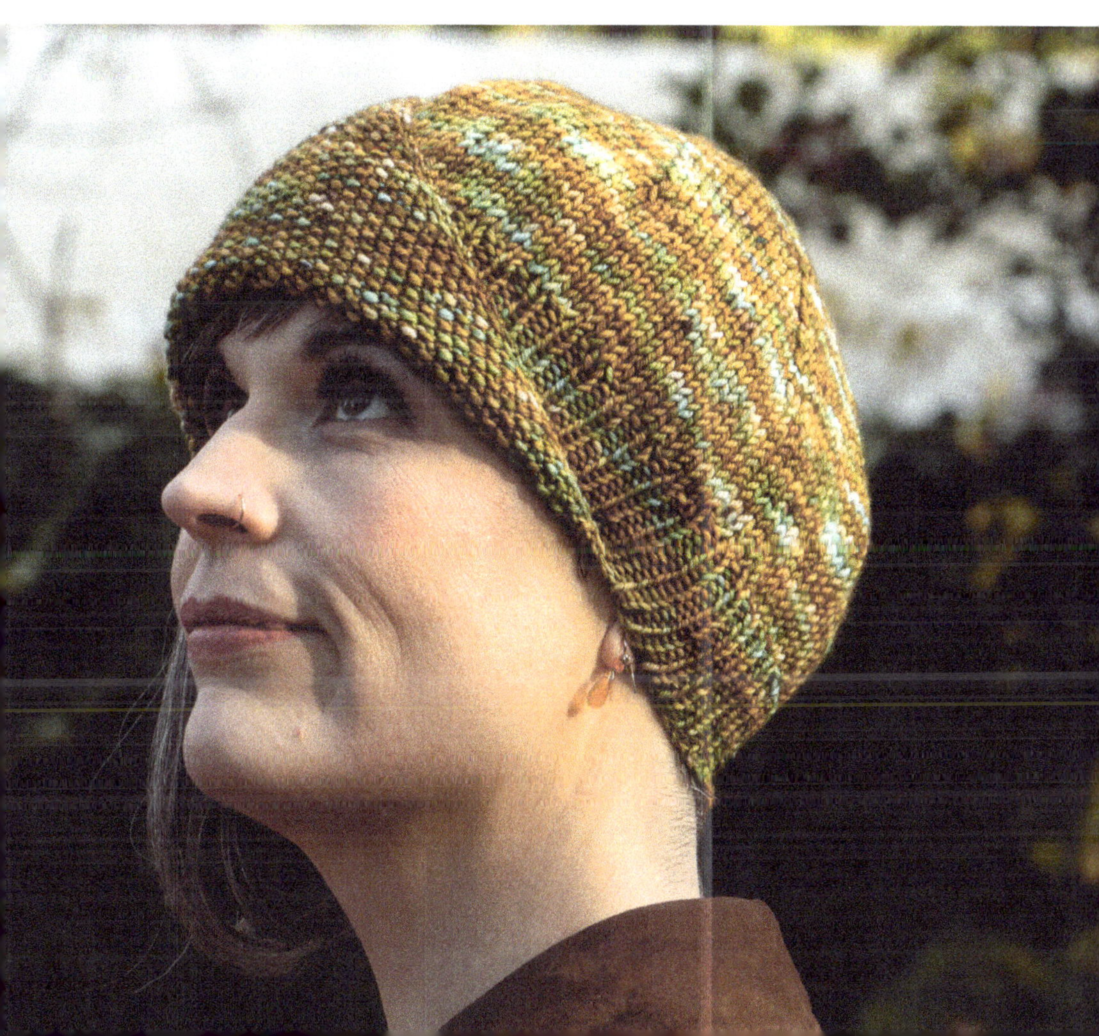

Hanks in the Hood

Rhodedendron, OR

Jen's love and appreciation for knitting started at a young age, wearing the knitted sweaters her grandmother made. She taught herself how to knit 17 years ago after the birth of her son. Then came her daughter, and a few years later she and her family left the city and moved to the boonies. After the move, Jen discovered the local yarn shop that had a knit night and it was there that she was introduced to spinning. From the moment she first watched others spinning she knew it was something that she had to do. The shop found a used Ashford traditional, gave Jen some wool and a how to book, and sent her home. Night after night Jen's husband would watch her swearing in frustration as she sat at the wheel trying to make something that somewhat resembled yarn. He questioned why she would want to try and do something that caused her so much anger! But slowly it started to click. Her hands and feet caught up to what her head knew she was supposed to do and she started to make yarn. She has been obsessed with the entire process ever since.

Website: www.mthoodyarnandwool.com
Shop: www.etsy.com/shop/hanksinthehood

Just as I was starting to pull together all the info for this profile, I was informed that Jen is headed off on her next adventure. It's not clear what the future holds, but I wouldn't be in the least bit surprised to see her back to dyeing lovely yarn in no time. I'd recommend keeping an eye on her etsy shop and website for updates.

Hanks in the Hood is located in Rhododendron, OR. I drew my inspiration from her location near the Barlow Road and the lovely conifer forests that cover the landscape. The Barlow Road Mitts are named for the last portion of the Oregon trail. This winding road brought settlers over Mt Hood and into the Willamette Valley. The road still exists in places and visitors can hike in the wheel ruts left by pioneer wagons. The mitts are knit from a rich pine colored yarn, aptly named "I Love Living in the Woods." A winding road complete with wheel ruts runs up the back of each hand.

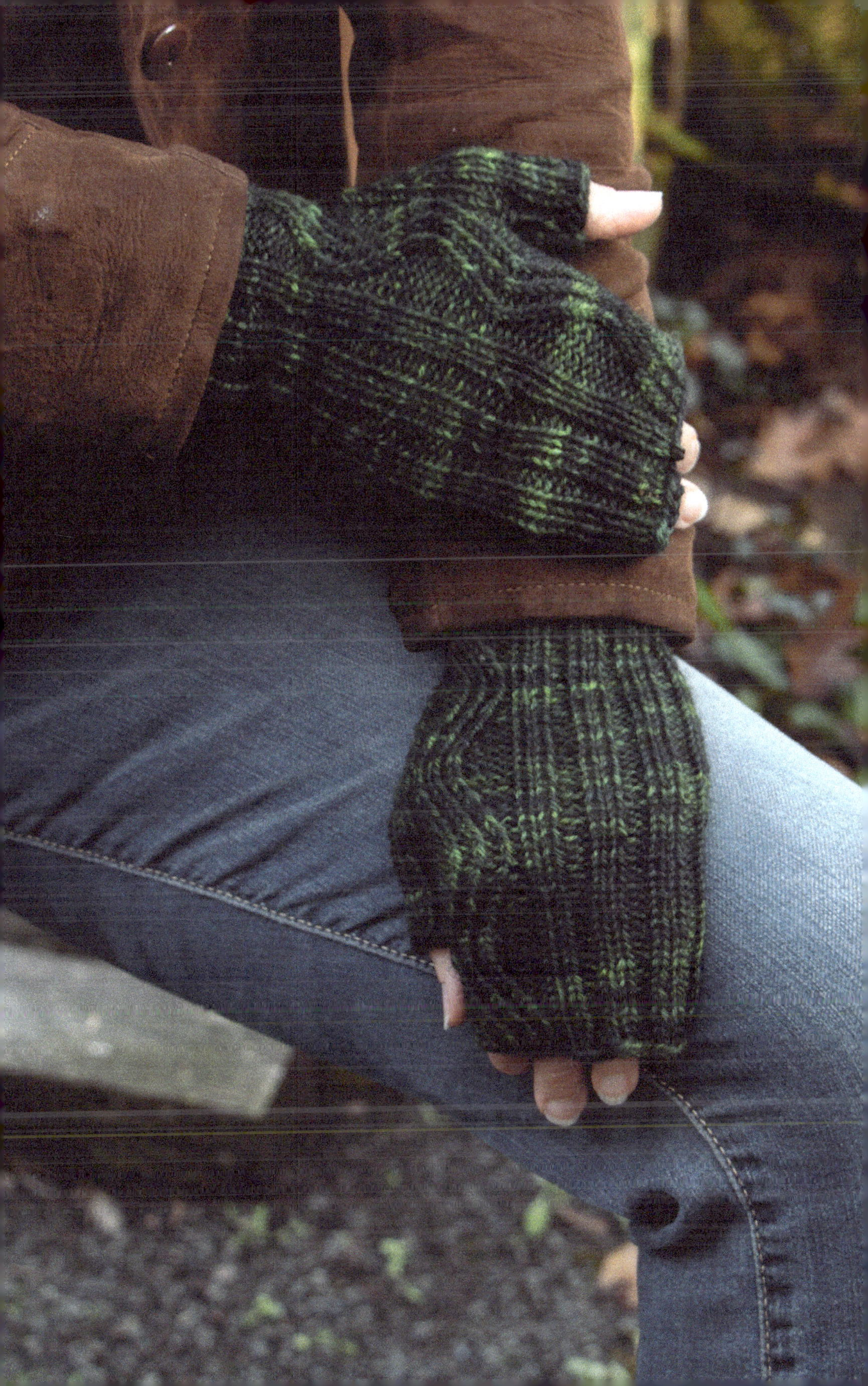

Barlow Road

FINISHED MEASURMENTS
Hand Circumference: 4.5 inches / 11.5cm (with tons of stretch)
Length: 9 inches / 23cm

YARN
150 yards / 137m of sport weight yarn

Yarn provided by Hanks in the Hood
100% Falkland Wool Sport
328 yards per 100g
Colorway: I Love Living in the Woods

OTHER MATERIALS
Set of 5 US size 4 (3.5mm) double pointed needles (or circular needle if magic loop is preferred) or size needed to obtain gauge

Scrap yarn or stitch holders

Cable needle

Tapestry needle

GAUGE
24 sts = 4 inches / 10cm in k2, p2 ribbing (unblocked and unstretched)

SPECIAL STITCHES
Right cross purl (rcp): Sl1 to the CN and hold in back, k1tbl, p1 from the CN.
Left cross purl (lcp): Sl1 to the CN and hold in front, p1, k1tbl from the CN

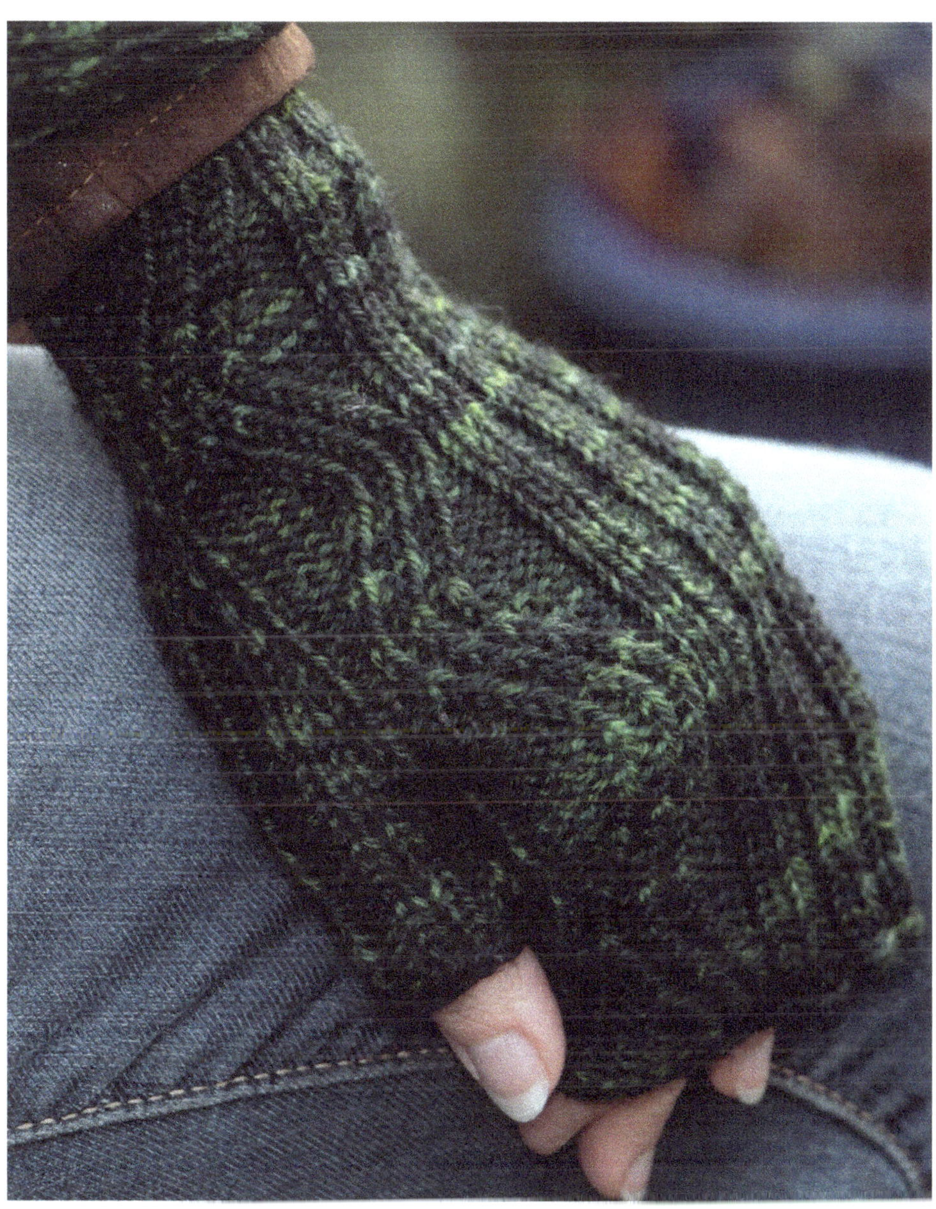

Pattern

Left Mitt
Cuff
CO 41 sts and join in the round taking care not to twist the work.

Set up rnd: K2, p1, k1, p1, k1, p1, k1 p5, *k2, p2, rep from * to end of rnd.

Rnd 1: K2, p1, k1tbl, p1, k1tbl, p1, k1tbl, p5, *k2, p2, rep from * to end of rnd.

Rep rnd 1 twice more (three reps total).

Rnd 2: K2, p1, lcp, lcp, lcp, p4, *k2, p2, rep from * to end of rnd.
Rnd 3: K2, p2, k1tbl, p1, k1tbl, p1, k1tbl, p4, *k2, p2, rep from * to end of rnd.
Rnd 4: K2, p2, lcp, lcp, lcp, p3, *k2, p2, rep from * to end of rnd.
Rnd 5: K2, p3, k1tbl, p1, k1tbl, p1, k1tbl, p3, *k2, p2, rep from * to end of rnd.
Rnd 6: K2, p3, lcp, lcp, lcp, p2, *k2, p2, rep from * to end of rnd.
Rnd 7: K2, p4, k1tbl, p1, k1tbl, p1, k1tbl, p2, *k2, p2, rep from * to end of rnd.
Rnd 8: K2, p4, lcp, lcp, lcp, p1, *k2, p2, rep from * to end of rnd.
Rnd 9: K2, p5, k1tbl, p1, k1tbl, p1, k1tbl, p1, *k2, p2, rep from * to end of rnd.
Rep rnd 9 twice more (three reps total).
Rnd 10: K2, p4, rcp, rcp, rcp, p1, *k2, p2, rep from * to end of rnd.
Rnd 11: K2, p4, k1tbl, p1, k1tbl, p1, k1tbl, p2, *k2, p2, rep from * to end of rnd.
Rnd 12: K2, p3, rcp, rcp, rcp, p2, *k2, p2, rep from * to end of rnd.
Rnd 13: K2, p3, k1tbl, p1, k1tbl, p1, k1tbl, p3, *k2, p2, rep from * to end of rnd.
Rnd 14: K2, p2, rcp, rcp, rcp, p3, *k2, p2, rep from * to end of rnd.
Rnd 15: K2, p2, k1tbl, p1, k1tbl, p1, k1tbl, p4, *k2, p2, rep from * to end of rnd.
Rnd 16: K2, p1, rcp, rcp, rcp, p4, *k2, p2, rep from * to end of rnd.
Rnd 17: K2, p1, k1tbl, p1, k1tbl, p1, k1tbl, p5, *k2, p2, rep from * to end of rnd.
Rep rnd 17 twice more (three reps total).

Gusset
Rnd 18: K2, p1, lcp, lcp, lcp, p4, *k2, p2, rep from * to end of rnd.
Rnd 19: K2, p2, k1tbl, p1, k1tbl, p1, k1tbl, p4, *k2, p2, rep from * to end of rnd.
Rnd 20: M1, k2, m1, p2, lcp, lcp, lcp, p3, *k2, p2, rep from * to end of rnd.
Rnd 21: K4, p3, k1tbl, p1, k1tbl, p1, k1tbl, p3, *k2, p2, rep from * to end of rnd.
Rnd 22: K4, p3, lcp, lcp, lcp, p2, *k2, p2, rep from * to end of rnd.
Rnd 23: K1, m1, k2, m1, k1, p4, k1tbl, p1, k1tbl, p1, k1tbl, p2, *k2, p2, rep from * to end of rnd.
Rnd 24: K1, p1, k2, p1, k1, p4, lcp, lcp, lcp, p1, *k2, p2, rep from * to end of rnd.
Rnd 25: K1, p1, k2, p1, k1, p5, k1tbl, p1, k1tbl, p1, k1tbl, p1, *k2, p2, rep from * to end of rnd.

Rnd 26: K1, m1, p1, k2, p1, m1, k1, p5, k1tbl, p1, k1tbl, p1, k1tbl, p1, *k2, p2, rep from * to end of rnd.
Rnd 27: K1, p2, k2, p2, k1, p5, k1tbl, p1, k1tbl, p1, k1tbl, p1, *k2, p2, rep from * to end of rnd.
Rnd 28: K1, p2, k2, p2, k1, p4, rcp, rcp, rcp, p1, *k2, p2, rep from * to end of rnd.
Rnd 29: K1, m1, p2, k2, p2, m1, k1, p4, k1tbl, p1, k1tbl, p1, k1tbl, p2, *k2, p2, rep from * to end of rnd.
Rnd 30: K2, p2, k2, p2, k2, p3, rcp, rcp, rcp, p2, *k2, p2, rep from * to end of rnd.
Rnd 31: K2, p2, k2, p2, k2, p3, k1tbl, p1, k1tbl, p1, k1tbl, p3, *k2, p2, rep from * to end of rnd.
Rnd 32: K1, m1, k1, p2, k2, p2, k1, m1, k1, p2, rcp, rcp, rcp, p3, *k2, p2, rep from * to end of rnd.
Rnd 33: K3, p2, k2, p2, k3, p2, k1tbl, p1, k1tbl, p1, k1tbl, p4, *k2, p2, rep from * to end of rnd.
Rnd 34: K3, p2, k2, p2, k3, p1, rcp, rcp, rcp, p4, *k2, p2, rep from * to end of rnd.
Rnd 35: K1, m1, k2, p2, k2, p2, k2, m1, k1, p1, k1tbl, p1, k1tbl, p1, k1tbl, p5, *k2, p2, rep from * to end of rnd.
Rnd 36: K1, p1, k2, p2, k2, p2, k2, p1, k1, p1, k1tbl, p1, k1tbl, p1, k1tbl, p5, *k2, p2, rep from * to end of rnd.
Rep rnd 36 once more (two reps total).
Rnd 37: K1, p1, k2, p2, k2, p2, k2, p1, k1, p1, lcp, lcp, lcp, p4, *k2, p2, rep from * to end of rnd.
Rnd 38: K1, p1, k2, p2, k2, p2, k2, p1, k1, p2, k1tbl, p1, k1tbl, p1, k1tbl, p4, *k2, p2, rep from * to end of rnd.
Rnd 39: K1, p1, k2, p2, k2, p2, k2, p1, k1, p2, lcp, lcp, lcp, p3, *k2, p2, rep from * to end of rnd.
Rnd 40: [K1, p1, k2, p2, k2, p2, k2, p1, k1] place these 14 sts on scrap yarn, using the backward loop method CO 2 sts, p5, k1tbl, p1, k1tbl, p1, k1tbl, p3, *k2, p2, rep from * to end of rnd.

Hand
Rnd 41: K2, p3, lcp, lcp, lcp, p2, *k2, p2, rep from * to end of rnd.
Rnd 42: K2, p4, k1tbl, p1, k1tbl, p1, k1tbl, p2, *k2, p2, rep from * to end of rnd.
Rnd 43: K2, p4, lcp, lcp, lcp, p1, *k2, p2, rep from * to end of rnd.
Rnd 44: K2, p5, k1tbl, p1, k1tbl, p1, k1tbl, p1, *k2, p2, rep from * to end of rnd.
Rep rnd 44 twice more (three reps total).
Rnd 45: K2, p4, rcp, rcp, rcp, p1, *k2, p2, rep from * to end of rnd.

Rnd 46: K2, p4, k1tbl, p1, k1tbl, p1, k1tbl, p2, *k2, p2, rep from * to end of rnd.
Rnd 47: K2, p3, rcp, rcp, rcp, p2, *k2, p2, rep from * to end of rnd.
Rnd 48: K2, p3, k1tbl, p1, k1tbl, p1, k1tbl, p3, *k2, p2, rep from * to end of rnd.
Rnd 49: K2, p2, rcp, rcp, rcp, p3, *k2, p2, rep from * to end of rnd.
Rnd 50: K2, p2, k1tbl, p1, k1tbl, p1, k1tbl, p4, *k2, p2, rep from * to end of rnd.
Rnd 51: K2, p1, rcp, rcp, rcp, p4, *k2, p2, rep from * to end of rnd.
Rnd 52: K2, p1, k1tbl, p1, k1tbl, p1, k1tbl, p5, *k2, p2, rep from * to end of rnd.
Rep rnd 52 twice more (three reps total).
Rnd 53: K2, p1, lcp, lcp, lcp, p4, *k2, p2, rep from * to end of rnd.
Rnd 54: K2, p2, k1tbl, p1, k1tbl, p1, k1tbl, p4, *k2, p2, rep from * to end of rnd.
Rnd 55: K2, p2, lcp, lcp, lcp, p3, *k2, p2, rep from * to end of rnd.
Rnd 56: K2, p3, k1tbl, p1, k1tbl, p1, k1tbl, p3, *k2, p2, rep from * to end of rnd.
Rep rnds 41 - 44 (including all three reps of rnd 44) once more.
Bind off all sts loosely.

Right Mitt

Cuff

CO 41 sts and join in the round taking care not to twist the work.
Set up rnd: K2, p5, k1, p1, k1, p1, k1 p1, *k2, p2, rep from * to end of rnd.
Rnd 1: K2, p5, k1tbl, p1, k1tbl, p1, k1tbl, p1, *k2, p2, rep from * to end of rnd.
Rep rnd 1 twice more (three reps total).
Rnd 2: K2, p4, rcp, rcp, rcp, p1, *k2, p2, rep from * to end of rnd.
Rnd 3: K2, p4, k1tbl, p1, k1tbl, p1, k1tbl, p2, *k2, p2, rep from * to end of rnd.
Rnd 4: K2, p3, rcp, rcp, rcp, p2, *k2, p2, rep from * to end of rnd.
Rnd 5: K2, p3, k1tbl, p1, k1tbl, p1, k1tbl, p3, *k2, p2, rep from * to end of rnd.
Rnd 6: K2, p2, rcp, rcp, rcp, p3, *k2, p2, rep from * to end of rnd.
Rnd 7: K2, p2, k1tbl, p1, k1tbl, p1, k1tbl, p4, *k2, p2, rep from * to end of rnd.
Rnd 8: K2, p1, rcp, rcp, rcp, p4, *k2, p2, rep from * to end of rnd.
Rnd 9: K2, p1, k1tbl, p1, k1tbl, p1, k1tbl, p5, *k2, p2, rep from * to end of rnd.

Rep rnd 9 twice more (three reps total).
Rnd 10: K2, p1, lcp, lcp, lcp, p4, *k2, p2, rep from * to end of rnd.
Rnd 11: K2, p2, k1tbl, p1, k1tbl, p1, k1tbl, p4, *k2, p2, rep from * to end of rnd.
Rnd 12: K2, p2, lcp, lcp, lcp, p3, *k2, p2, rep from * to end of rnd.
Rnd 13: K2, p3, k1tbl, p1, k1tbl, p1, k1tbl, p3, *k2, p2, rep from * to end of rnd.
Rnd 14: K2, p3, lcp, lcp, lcp, p2, *k2, p2, rep from * to end of rnd.
Rnd 15: K2, p4, k1tbl, p1, k1tbl, p1, k1tbl, p2, *k2, p2, rep from * to end of rnd.
Rnd 16: K2, p4, lcp, lcp, lcp, p1, *k2, p2, rep from * to end of rnd.
Rnd 17: K2, p5, k1tbl, p1, k1tbl, p1, k1tbl, p1, *k2, p2, rep from * to end of rnd.
Rep rnd 17 twice more (three reps total).

Gusset
Rnd 18: K2, p4, rcp, rcp, rcp, p1, *k2, p2, rep from * to end of rnd.
Rnd 19: K2, p4, k1tbl, p1, k1tbl, p1, k1tbl, p2, *k2, p2, rep from * to end of rnd.
Rnd 20: K2, p3, rcp, rcp, rcp, p2, m1, k2, m1, p2, *k2, p2, rep from * to end of rnd.
Rnd 21: K2, p3, k1tbl, p1, k1tbl, p1, k1tbl, p3, k4, p2,*k2, p2, rep from * to end of rnd.
Rnd 22: K2, p2, rcp, rcp, rcp, p3, k4, p2, *k2, p2, rep from * to end of rnd.
Rnd 23: K2, p2, k1tbl, p1, k1tbl, p1, k1tbl, p4, k1, m1, k2, m1, k1, p2, *k2, p2, rep from * to end of rnd.
Rnd 24: K2, p1, rcp, rcp, rcp, p4, k1, p1, k2, p1, k1, p2, *k2, p2, rep from * to end of rnd.
Rnd 25: K2, p1, k1tbl, p1, k1tbl, p1, k1tbl, p5, k1, p1, k2, p1, k1, p2, *k2, p2, rep from * to end of rnd.
Rnd 26: K2, p1, k1tbl, p1, k1tbl, p1, k1tbl, p5, k1, m1, p1, k2, p1, m1, k1, p2, *k2, p2, rep from * to end of rnd.
Rnd 27: K2, p1, k1tbl, p1, k1tbl, p1, k1tbl, p5, k1, p2, k2, p2, k1, p2, *k2, p2, rep from * to end of rnd.
Rnd 28: K2, p1, lcp, lcp, lcp, p4, k1, p2, k2, p2, k1, p2, *k2, p2, rep from * to end of rnd.
Rnd 29: K2, p2, k1tbl, p1, k1tbl, p1, k1tbl, p4, k1, m1, p2, k2, p2, m1, k1, p2, *k2, p2, rep from * to end of rnd.
Rnd 30: K2, p2, lcp, lcp, lcp, p3, k2, p2, k2, p2, k2, p2, *k2, p2, rep from * to end of rnd.
Rnd 31: K2, p3, k1tbl, p1, k1tbl, p1, k1tbl, p3, k2, p2, k2, p2, k2, p2, *k2, p2, rep from * to end of rnd.

Rnd 32: K2, p3, lcp, lcp, lcp, p2, k1, m1, k1, p2, k2, p2, k1, m1, k1, p2, *k2, p2, rep from* to end of rnd.
Rnd 33: K2, p4, k1tbl, p1, k1tbl, p1, k1tbl, p2, k3, p2, k2, p2, k3, p2, *k2, p2, rep from * to end of rnd.
Rnd 34: K2, p4, lcp, lcp, lcp, p1, k3, p2, k2, p2, k3, p2, *k2, p2, rep from * to end of rnd.
Rnd 35: K2, p5, k1tbl, p1, k1tbl, p1, k1tbl, p1, k1, m1, k2, p2, k2, p2, k2, m1, k1, p2, *k2, p2, rep from * to end of rnd.
Rnd 36: K2, p5, k1tbl, p1, k1tbl, p1, k1tbl, p1, k1, p1, k2, p2, k2, p2, k2, p1, k1, p2, *k2, p2, rep from * to end of rnd.
Rep rnd 36 once more (two reps total).
Rnd 37: K2, p4, rcp, rcp, rcp, p1, k1, p1, k2, p2, k2, p2, k2, p1, k1, p2, *k2, p2, rep from * to end of rnd.
Rnd 38: K2, p4, k1tbl, p1, k1tbl, p1, k1tbl, p2, k1, p1, k2, p2, k2, p2, k2, p1, k1, p2, *k2, p2, rep from * to end of rnd.
Rnd 39: K2, p3, rcp, rcp, rcp, p2, k1, p1, k2, p2, k2, p2, k2, p1, k1, p2, *k2, p2, rep from * to end of rnd.
Rnd 40: K2, p3, k1tbl, p1, k1tbl, p1, k1tbl, p3, [k1, p1, k2, p2, k2, p2, k2, p1, k1] place these 14 sts on scrap yarn, using the backward loop method CO 2 sts, p2, *k2, p2, rep from * to end of rnd.

Hand
Rnd 41: K2, p2, rcp, rcp, rcp, p3, *k2, p2, rep from * to end of rnd.
Rnd 42: K2, p2, k1tbl, p1, k1tbl, p1, k1tbl, p4, *k2, p2, rep from * to end of rnd.
Rnd 43: K2, p1, rcp, rcp, rcp, p4, *k2, p2, rep from * to end of rnd.
Rnd 44: K2, p1, k1tbl, p1, k1tbl, p1, k1tbl, p5, *k2, p2, rep from * to end of rnd.
Rep rnd 44 twice more (three reps total).
Rnd 45: K2, p1, lcp, lcp, lcp, p4, *k2, p2, rep from * to end of rnd.
Rnd 46: K2, p2, k1tbl, p1, k1tbl, p1, k1tbl, p4, *k2, p2, rep from * to end of rnd.
Rnd 47: K2, p2, lcp, lcp, lcp, p3, *k2, p2, rep from * to end of rnd.
Rnd 48: K2, p3, k1tbl, p1, k1tbl, p1, k1tbl, p3, *k2, p2, rep from * to end of rnd.
Rnd 49: K2, p3, lcp, lcp, lcp, p2, *k2, p2, rep from * to end of rnd.
Rnd 50: K2, p4, k1tbl, p1, k1tbl, p1, k1tbl, p2, *k2, p2, rep from * to end of rnd.
Rnd 51: K2, p4, lcp, lcp, lcp, p1, *k2, p2, rep from * to end of rnd.
Rnd 52: K2, p5, k1tbl, p1, k1tbl, p1, k1tbl, p1, *k2, p2, rep from * to end of rnd.

Rep rnd 52 twice more (three reps total).
Rnd 53: K2, p4, rcp, rcp, rcp, p1, *k2, p2, rep from * to end of rnd.
Rnd 54: K2, p4, k1tbl, p1, k1tbl, p1, k1tbl, p2, *k2, p2, rep from * to end of rnd.
Rnd 55: K2, p3, rcp, rcp, rcp, p2, *k2, p2, rep from * to end of rnd.
Rnd 56: K2, p3, k1tbl, p1, k1tbl, p1, k1tbl, p3, *k2, p2, rep from * to end of rnd.
Rep ends 41 - 44 (including all three reps of rnd 44) once more.
Bind off all sts loosely.

THUMB (both hands)
Set Up Rnd: Place the 14 sts from the scrap yarn onto 2 needles. With the 3rd needle and working from the right side, pick up 2 sts from the cast on edge at the hand.
Work p2, k2 ribbing for 1 inch / 2.5cm (or desired thumb height).
Bind off all sts loosely.

Weave in ends. To preserve the three dimensional texture and stretchiness of the ribbing, do not block the mitts.

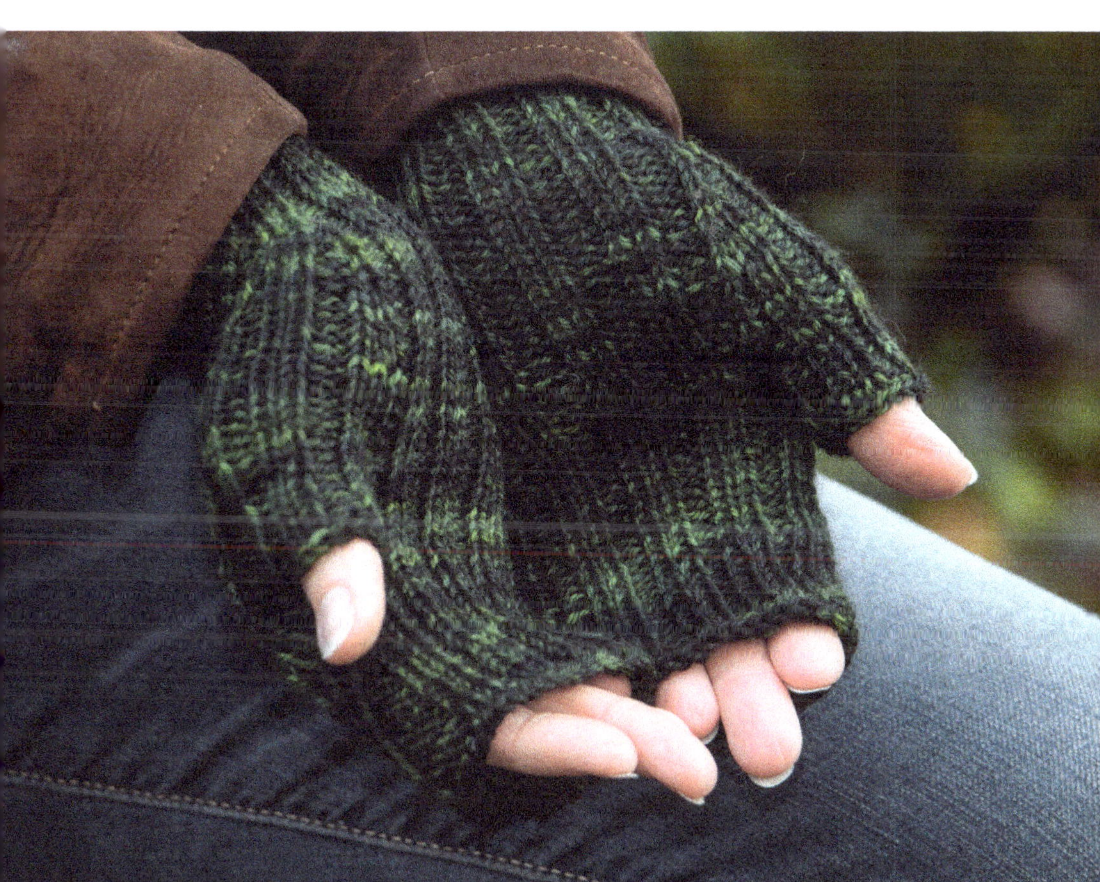

Fierce Fibers

Hillsboro, OR

Stacey is a 30 something mother of 3 living on a tree farm outside of Portland, Oregon. Originally from a suburb of Buffalo, NY, she moved to Oregon in 2005 with her husband. Stacey went to the State University of New York at Buffalo for her undergraduate degree in physics, followed by the University of Leiden in The Netherlands for her graduate degree in applied physics. She worked a corporate job for a while after she graduated, but after her second son was born she left her career in semiconductor technology to take care of her family.

Stacey learned how to knit out of frustration, looking for something project based to work on while at home with her children. After learning how to knit at a big box store, she discovered Ravelry, made the best knitting friends, and expanded her fiber knowledge. She decided to give dyeing a try when a local yarn shop owner approached her to dye something special for an event they were having. Stacey became infatuated with learning the different dye chemistries and exploring her own color sense. This led to falling down the rabbit hole and she now owns knitting machines and makes her own dye blanks. Maintaining and owning knitting machines allows her to exercise her engineering brain while the dyeing keeps her creative. The synergy of the two are the soul of her business.

If engineering and dyeing are the soul of Fierce Fibers then heritage is the heart. Stacey believes we are what we have left behind. This is why she tries to create yarn that would be befitting of an heirloom item, knowing there is so much more to knitting than just making an item to wear or to look at. We craft with love and we put that love in our items, so why use yarn that wasn't made with the same intention? This is what drives her every day at Fierce Fibers....keep it real, keep it kind and keep doing you!

Website: www.fiercefibers.com
Instagram: @fiercefibers
Email: fiberista@fiercefibers.com

I have to start by pointing out how truly awesome the Fierce Fibers tag line is: "Luxury fibers for both your inner princess and outer warrior." That's some seriously badass yarn.

When Stacey and I were getting to know each other I asked her where she lived. Her reply included the comment, "Quite a drive but I have chickens and a garden." Without any doubt I knew in that moment that the name of the pattern I designed for her had to be, "I have Chickens." The brioche cowl I settled on features chicken eggs hidden in the grass with cute little chicken feet on both edges. Stacey's signature gradient yarn gives the project that extra special touch.

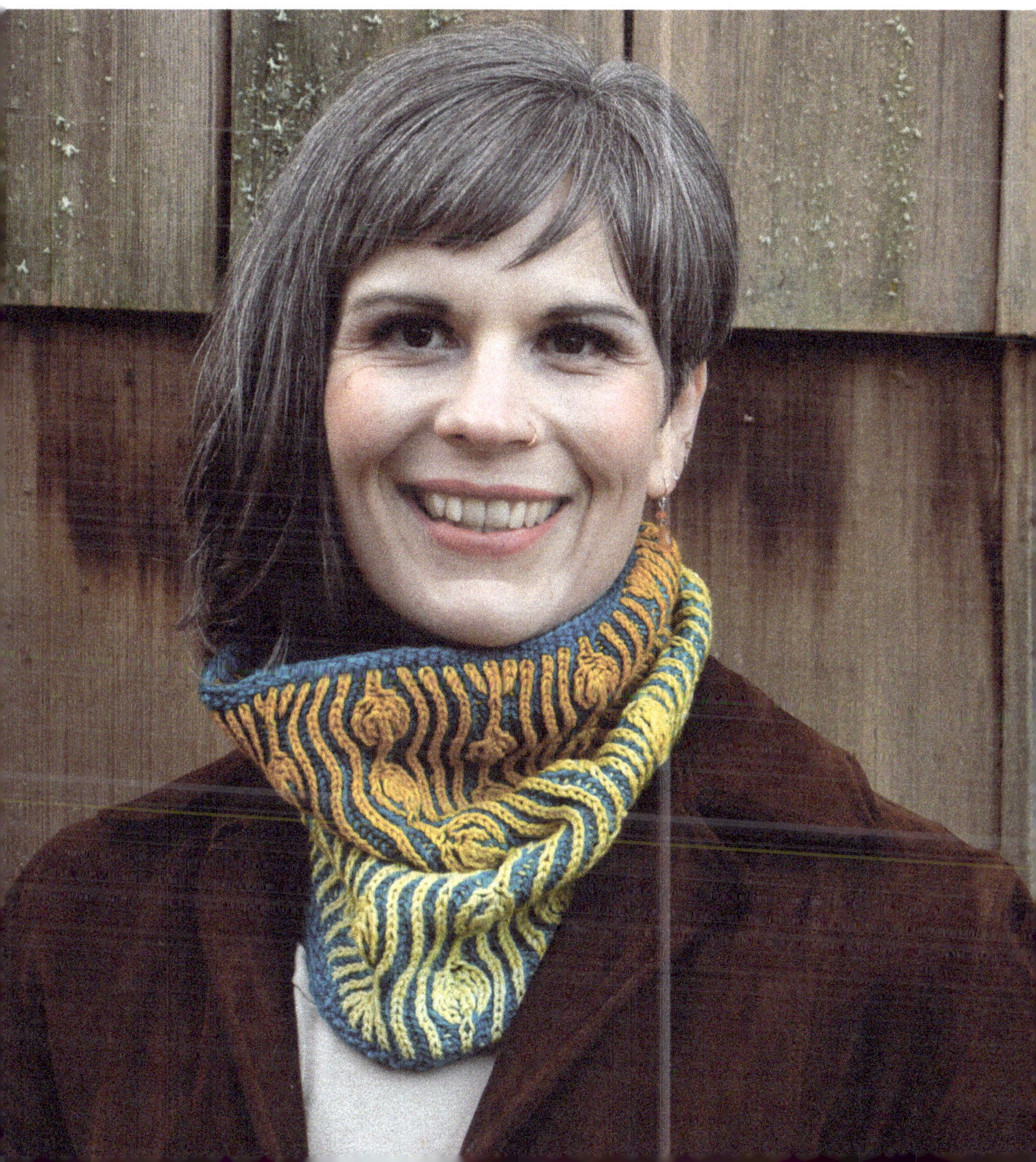

I Have Chickens

FINISHED MEASURMENTS
Circumference: 22 inches / 56cm
Height: 12 inches / 30cm (easily adjustable)

YARN
225 yards / 205m each of two colors of fingering weight yarn

Yarn provided by Fierce Fibers
True: 80% superwash merino, 20% nylon
400 yards per 115g
Main Color (MC): Preen
Contrast Color (CC): Free Range (gradient)

OTHER MATERIALS
US size 4 (3.5mm) 24 inch / 60cm circular needle or size needed to obtain gauge

Removable stitch marker

Stitch marker

Tapestry needle

GAUGE
22 sts = 4 inches / 10cm in seed stitch

Brk (brioche knit): knit the stitch together with its yarn over

Brp (brioche purl): purl the stitch together with its yarn over

Sl1yo (slip 1 yarn over): With the yarn in front, slip the stitch purlwise and bring the yarn over the needle. The slipped stitch with its yo are considered one stitch.

Br4st dec (brioche 4 st decrease): This is a centered decrease worked over 5 sts. You will need a removable stitch marker.
1: Slip the first brioche st knitwise with its yarn over.
2: Slip the next st knitwise.
3: Place the next brioche st with its yarn over onto the removable marker and hold in the front of the work.
4: Knit the next st on the LH needle and pass the last slipped st over the knit st.
5: Slip the knit st to the LH needle purlwise and pass the next brioche st over the knit st.
6: Move the knit st to the RH needle purlwise and pass the first slipped brioche st over the knit st.
7: Move the brioche st from the marker to the LH needle.
8: Slip the knit st to the LH needle purlwise and pass previously held brioche sts over.
9: Move the knit st back to RH needle purlwise.

Br4st inc (brioche 4 st increase): Brk without dropping the st off the LH needle, yo, brk into the same stitch again without dropping it off the needle, yo, brk on more time, now dropping the st off the needle. Five sts made from 1 st.

Pattern

With the MC CO 120 sts. Join in the round taking care not to twist the work and place a marker to indicate the end of the rnd.

Rnd 1: *K1, p1, rep from * to end of rnd.

Rnd 2: *P1, k1, rep from * to end of rnd.

Rep rnd 1 once more.

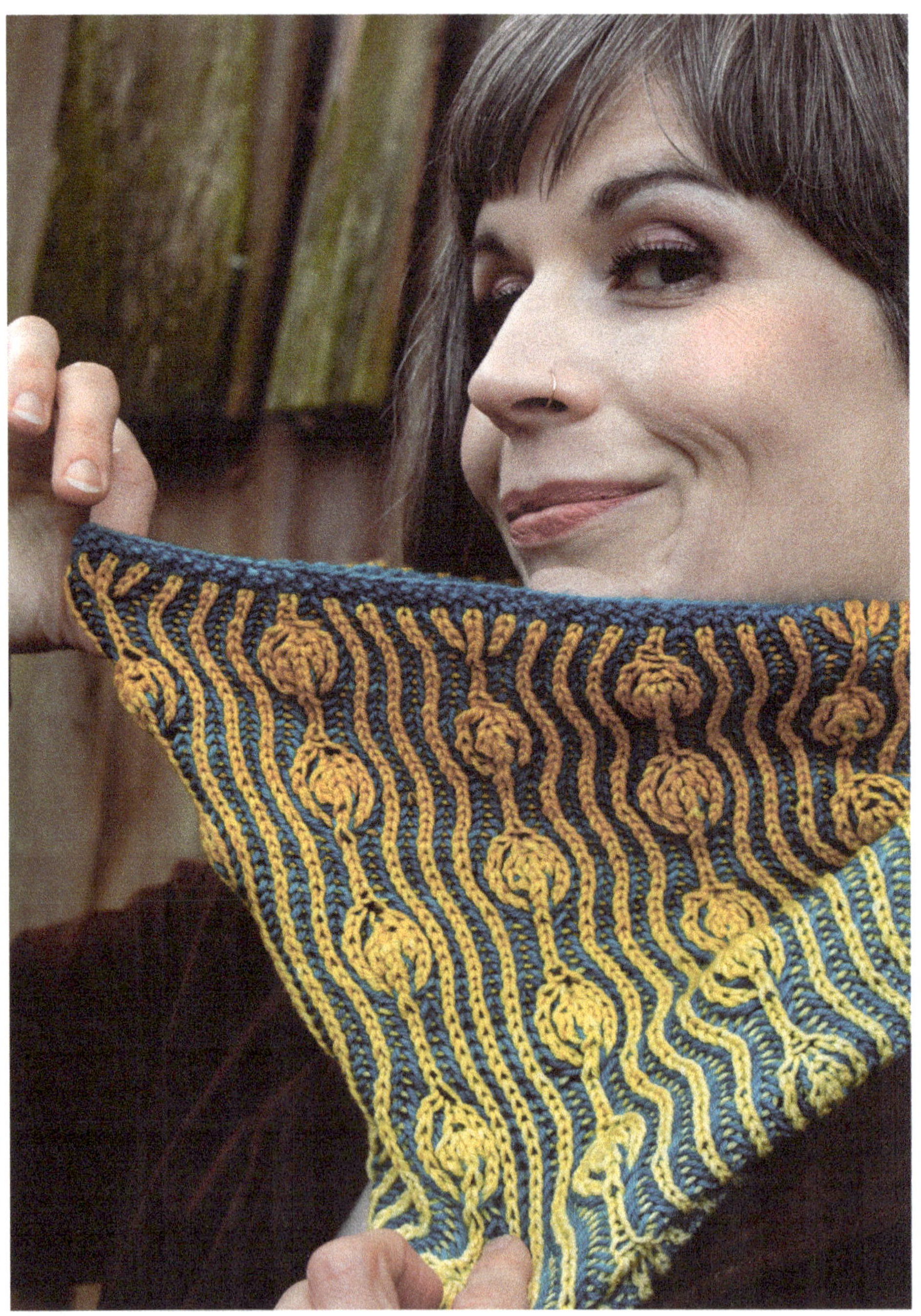

Rnd 3: With CC *Sl1yo, k1, rep from * to end of rnd.
Rnd 4: With MC *Brp1, sl1yo, rep from * to end of rnd.
Rnd 5: With CC *Sl1yo, brk1, rep from * to end of rnd.
Repeat rnds 4 and 5 twice more (three reps total).
Rnd 6 and all even rnds: With MC *Brp1, sl1yo, rep from * to end of rnd.
All odd rnds are worked with the CC.
Rnd 7: *Sl1yo, br4st dec, [sl1yo, brk1] three times, sl1yo, br4st inc,
[sl1yo, brk1] three times, rep from * to end of rnd.
Rnd 9: *Sl1yo, brk1, rep from * to end of rnd.
Rnd 11: *[Sl1yo, brk1] five times, sl1yo, br4st inc, [sl1yo, brk1] four
times, rep from * to end of rnd.
Rnds 13 and 15: *Sl1yo, brk1, rep from * to end of rnd.
Rnd 17: *[Sl1yo, brk1] five times, sl1yo, br4st dec, [sl1yo, brk1] four
times, rep from * to end of rnd.
Rnd 19: *Sl1yo, brk1, rep from * to end of rnd.
Rnd 21: *Sl1yo, br4st inc, [sl1yo, brk1] three times, sl1yo, br4st dec,
[sl1yo, brk1] three times, rep from * to end of rnd.
Rnd 23: *Sl1yo, brk1, rep from * to end of rnd.
Rnd 25: *Sl1yo, brk1, sl1yo, br4st inc, [sl1yo, brk1] eight times, rep from
* to end of rnd.
Rnd 27 and 29: *Sl1yo, brk1, rep from * to end of rnd.
Rnd 31: *Sl1yo, brk1, sl1yo, br4st dec, [sl1yo, brk1] eight times, rep from
* to end of rnd.
Rnd 33: *Sl1yo, brk1, rep from * to end of rnd.
Rep rnds 6 - 33 four more times (five
reps total). Add or subtract reps as
desired to adjust the cowl height.
Rep rnds 6 - 23 once.
Rnd 34: With MC *Brp1, sl1yo, rep from
* to end of rnd.
Rnd 35: With CC *Sl1yo, brk1, rep from *
to end of rnd.
Rep rnds 34 and 35 once more (two reps
total).
Rnd 36: With MC *Brk1, k1, rep from *
to end of rnd.
Rnd 37: *K1, p1, rep from * to end of
rnd.
Rnd 38: *P1, k1, rep from * to end of rnd.
Rep rnd 37 once more.
BO all sts loosely.
Weave in ends and block to shape.

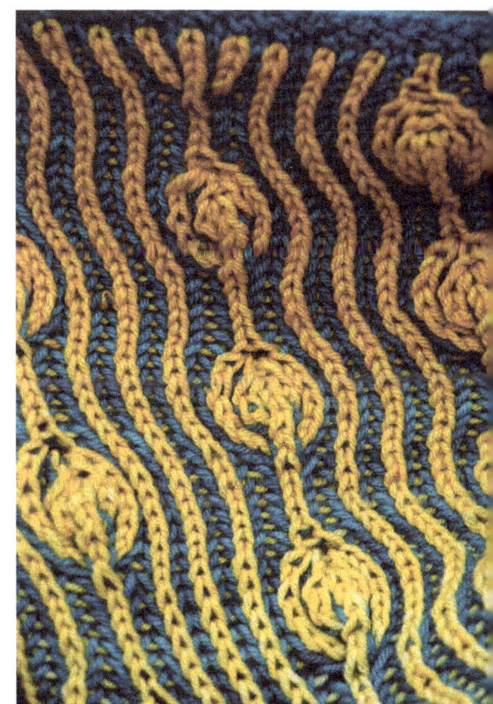

Henlia Handmade

Bend, OR

Henlia Handmade started one day when Mindy stumbled across an article about how badly dyes used in the commercial dyeing process pollute our waterways. She wanted to do something about it, so she set out to create the most delicious yarn for the most eco-conscious knitters and crocheters in the fiber community. By sourcing ethically harvested dye materials and even growing some of her own, Mindy's naturally dyed yarn helps keep our water sources clean and uses far fewer natural resources to create.

It turns out the road was more difficult than Mindy had imagined. She struggled to balance caring for two young children (ages 1 and 3-1/2) while learning a new skill and starting a business, and, of course, maintaining her relationship with her husband. While her children were distracted she found pockets of time to work. Her husband also stepped in, whisking the kids away on grocery errands after his long days at work so that Mindy could have more time.

And then there was the task of finding just the right U.S. wool to use. Wow. That one was a toughie! Finding a yarn base took trial and error. Mindy bought many samples from ranches and mills as near as down the road to as far away as the opposite coast. Supporting U.S. wool was critical to her mission not only for the sake of humane animal practices, but also because she feels it is important to support small businesses within her community and her country.

But, despite all these hurdles, when she released her first product line collection the response was overwhelmingly supportive. There is a market for naturally dyed and responsibly sourced yarn and Henlia Handmade helps fill that need.

Website: www.henliahandmade.com
Shop: www.etsy.com/shop/henliahandmade
Instagram: @henliahandmade
Facebook: Henlia Handmade
Email: hello@henliahandmade.com (general inquiries)
info@henliahandmade.com (wholesale inquiries)

I was inspired by Mindy's commitment to using ethically sourced
natural dyes and locally raised wool. Anything I designed with her
yarn had to reflect the natural world from which it came. I settled
on a tam with a single large flower encircled with small leaves. The
design echoes the plant material that was used to dye the yarn. I'd
never knit with rambouillet fiber before and it was a lot of fun getting
to know with this wonderfully soft, springy yarn.

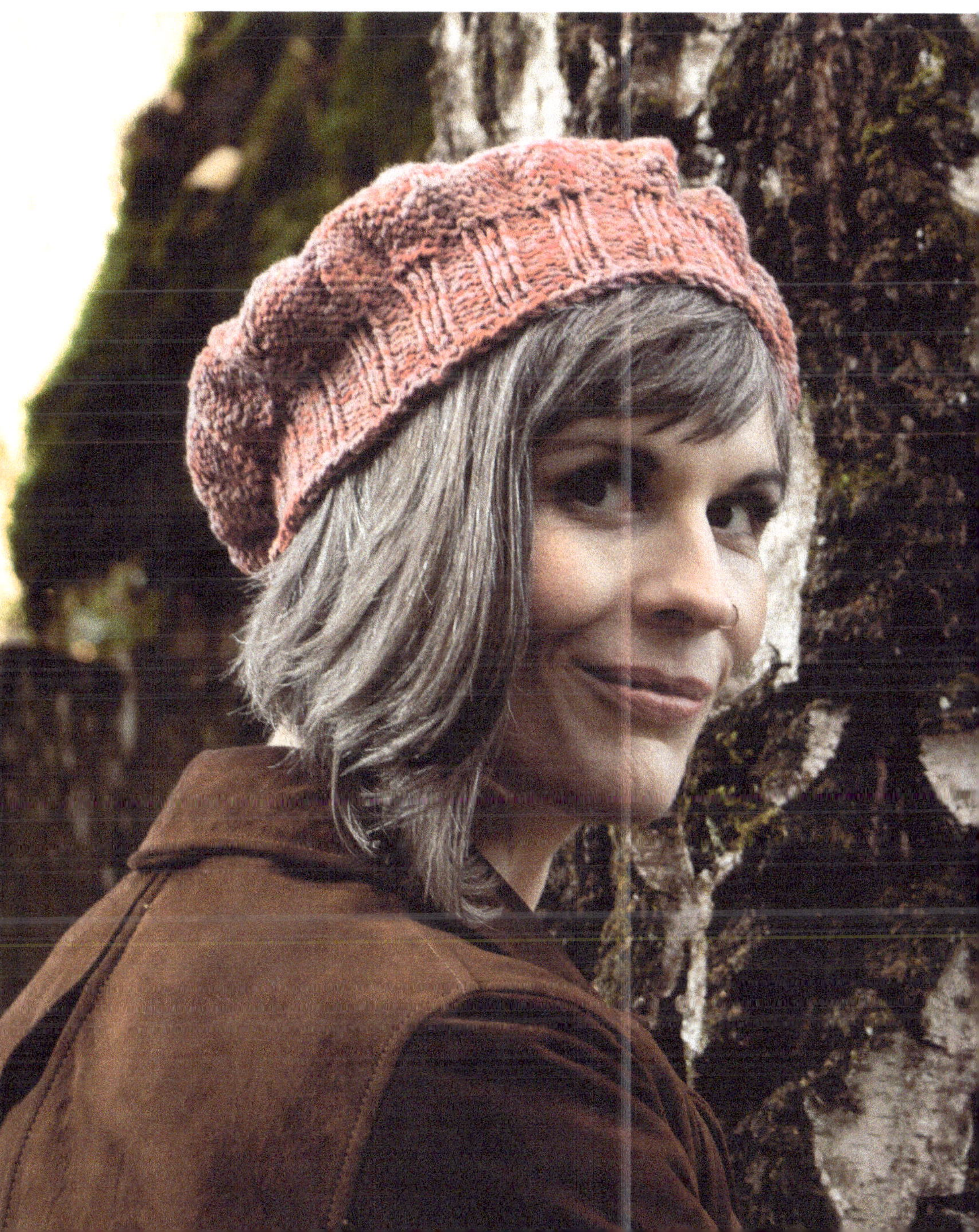

Late Harvest

FINISHED MEASURMENTS
Circumference: 16 inches / 41cm (Has plenty of stretch for larger heads.)

YARN
150 yards / 137m of worsted weight yarn

Yarn provided by Henlia Handmade
2ply Worsted Weight: 100% US rambouillet
200 yards per 100g
Colorway: Enchanting Fall

OTHER MATERIALS
Set of 5 US Size 8 (5mm) double pointed needles (or circular needle if magic loop is preferred) or size needed to obtain gauge
Set of 5 US Size 5 (3.75mm) double pointed needles (or circular needle if magic loop is preferred)

Tapestry needle

GAUGE
17 sts = 4 inches / 10cm in stockinette stitch on larger needles.

PATTERN

With the larger needles CO 8 sts onto one needle.

Rnd 1: Starting with the first cast on stitch and bringing the working yarn across the back as for an i-cord, knit 2 sts onto the first dpn, switch to the second dpn and k2. Continue adding dpns until all the stitches have been worked and are distributed 2 sts per needle.

Rnd 2: P8.

Each odd rnd will add 8 sts.

Rnd 3: *M1, k1, rep from * to end of rnd.

Rnd 4: P16.

Rnd 5: [K1, yo, k1, yo, k1, p1] four times.

Rnd 6: [K5, p1] four times.

Rnd 7: [K1, yo, k3, yo, k1, p1] four times.

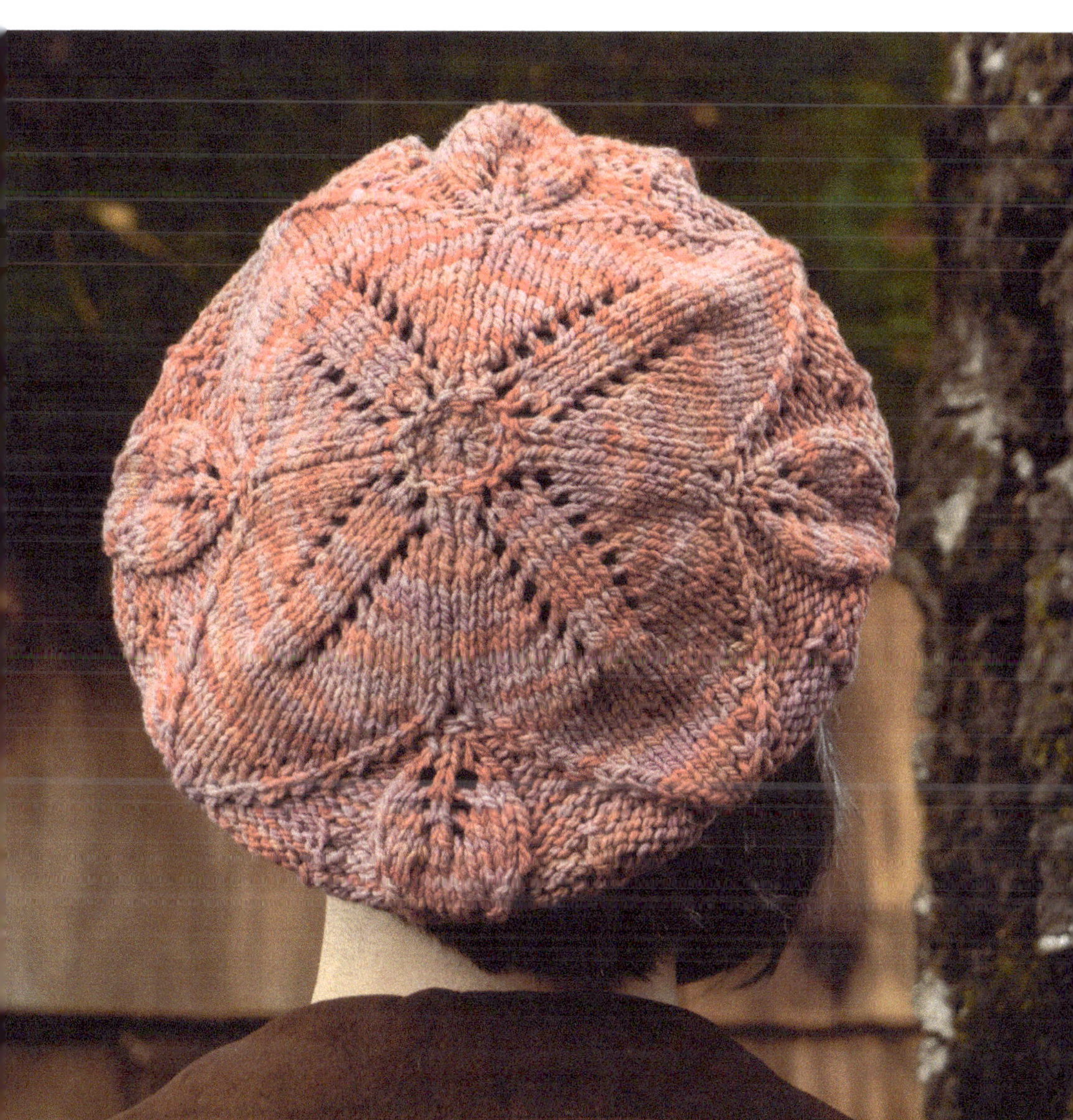

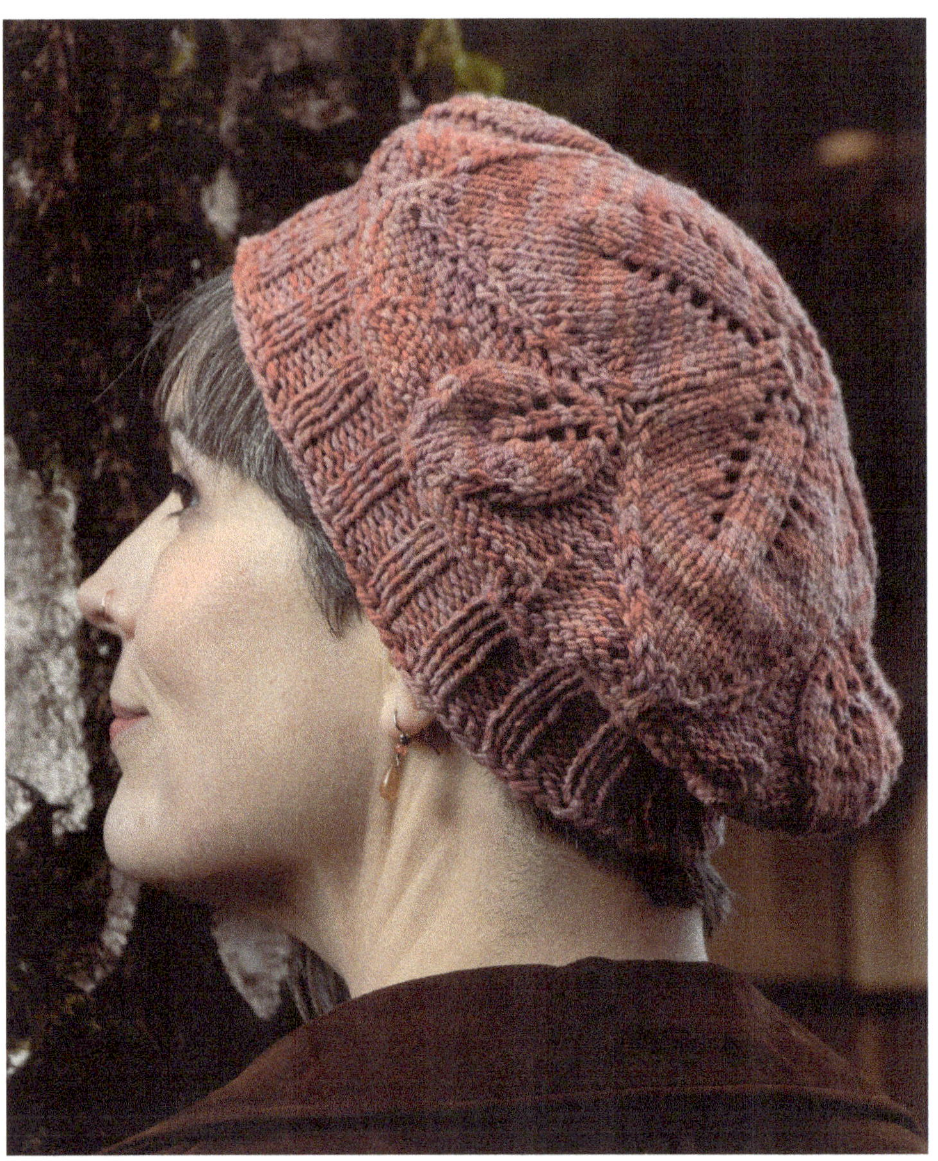

Rnd 8: [K7, p1] four times.
Rnd 9: [K2, yo, k3, yo, k2, p1] four times.
Rnd 10: [K9, p1] four times.
Rnd 11: [K3, yo, k3, yo, k3, p1] four times.
Rnd 12: [K11, p1] four times.
Rnd 13: [K4, yo, k3, yo, k4, p1] four times.
Rnd 14: [K13, p1] four times.
Rnd 15: [K5, yo, k3, yo, k5, p1] four times.
Rnd 16: [K15, p1] four times.
Rnd 17: [K6, yo, k3, yo, k6, p1] four times.
Rnd 18: [K17, p1] four times.

Rnd 19: [K7, yo, k3, yo, k7, p1] four times.
Rnd 20: [K19, p1] four times.
Rnd 21: [M1, ssk, k6, yo, k3, yo, k6, k2tog, m1, k1] four times.
Rnd 22: [P1, k19, p1, k1] four times.
Rnd 23: [P1, m1, ssk, k15, k2tog, m1, p1, m1, k1, m1] four times.
Rnd 24: [P2, k17, p2, k3] four times.
Row 25: [P2, m1, ssk, k13, k2tog, m1, p2, k1, yo, k1, yo, k1] four times.
Row 26: [P3, k15, p3, k5] four times.
Row 27: [P3, m1, ssk, k11, k2tog, m1, p3, k2, yo, k1, yo, k2] four times.
Row 28: [P4, k13, p4, k7] four times.
Row 29: [P4, m1, ssk, k9, k2tog, m1, p4, k3, yo, k1, yo, k3] four times.
Row 30: [P5, k11, p5, k9] four times.
Row 31: [P5, m1, ssk, k7, k2tog, m1, p5, k4, yo, k1, yo, k4] four times.
Row 32: [P6, k9, p6, k11] four times.
Row 33: [M1, p3, m1, p3, m1, ssk, k5, k2tog, m1, p3, m1, p3, m1, ssk, k7, k2tog] four times.
Row 34: [P9, k7, p9, k9] four times.
Row 35: [M1, p4, m1, p5, m1, ssk, k3, k2tog, m1, p5, m1, p4, m1, ssk, k5, k2tog] four times.
Row 36: [P12, k5, p12, k7] four times.
Row 37: [M1, p6, m1, p6, m1, ssk, k1, k2tog, m1, p6, m1, p6, m1, ssk, k3, k2tog] four times.
Row 38: [P15, k3, p15, k5] four times.
Row 39: [M1, p7, m1, p8, m1, cdd, m1, p8, m1, p7, m1, ssk, k1, k2tog] four times.
Row 40: [P37, k3] four times.
Row 41: [M1, p11, m1, p15, m1, p11, m1, cdd] four times. - 168 sts
Row 42: Purl all sts.
Row 43: *P2, p2tog, rep from * to end of rnd. - 126 sts
Row 44: Purl all sts.
Row 45: *P2tog, p1, rep from * to end of rnd. - 84 sts
Switch to smaller needles.
Row 46: *K2, p2, rep from * to end of rnd.
Rep rnd 46 until you have 2 inches / 5cm of ribbing.
BO all sts as follows:
K2, insert the tip of the LH needle into the front of the 2 sts on the RH needle, knit the 2 together through the back loops, *k1, insert the tip of the LH needle into the front of the 2 sts on the RH needle, knit the 2 together through the back loops, rep from * until all sts are bound off.
Weave in ends and block to shape.

Three Fates Yarns

Salem, OR

Stephania has been dyeing yarn and fiber as Three Fates Yarns since 2008. She specializes in dyeing semi-solid yarns in a wide range of colors. Her lifelong obsession with color can be seen in the broad palette of rich colors that she offers. She loves making all sorts of things and can usually be found working on a pair of socks or a sweater, or spinning yarn.

When naming her business, Stephania drew from Greek mythology. The Three Fates are traditionally referred to as the Spinner, the Weaver, and the Cutter. In literature they have frequently been reimagined as women in three phases of life, Maiden, Mother, and Crone. As greek goddesses, they control the fate of human lives; literally spinning the thread of life, weaving a tapestry of life's journal, and ending it with a snip. Stephania likes to imagine them as goddesses of the fiber arts, though they predate knitting.

Website: www.threefatesyarns.com
Instagram: @threefatesyarns
Email: threefatesyarns@gmail.com

It was Stephania's "day job" that gave me the inspiration for her design. She has a Master's in Environmental Law and works as a sustainability analyst at Portland Community College. Her passion for social justice, equity, and inclusion led me to create a shawl with equal sized sections, each using one of her glorious colors. This is a perfect project for those mini-skeins that you just can't resist.

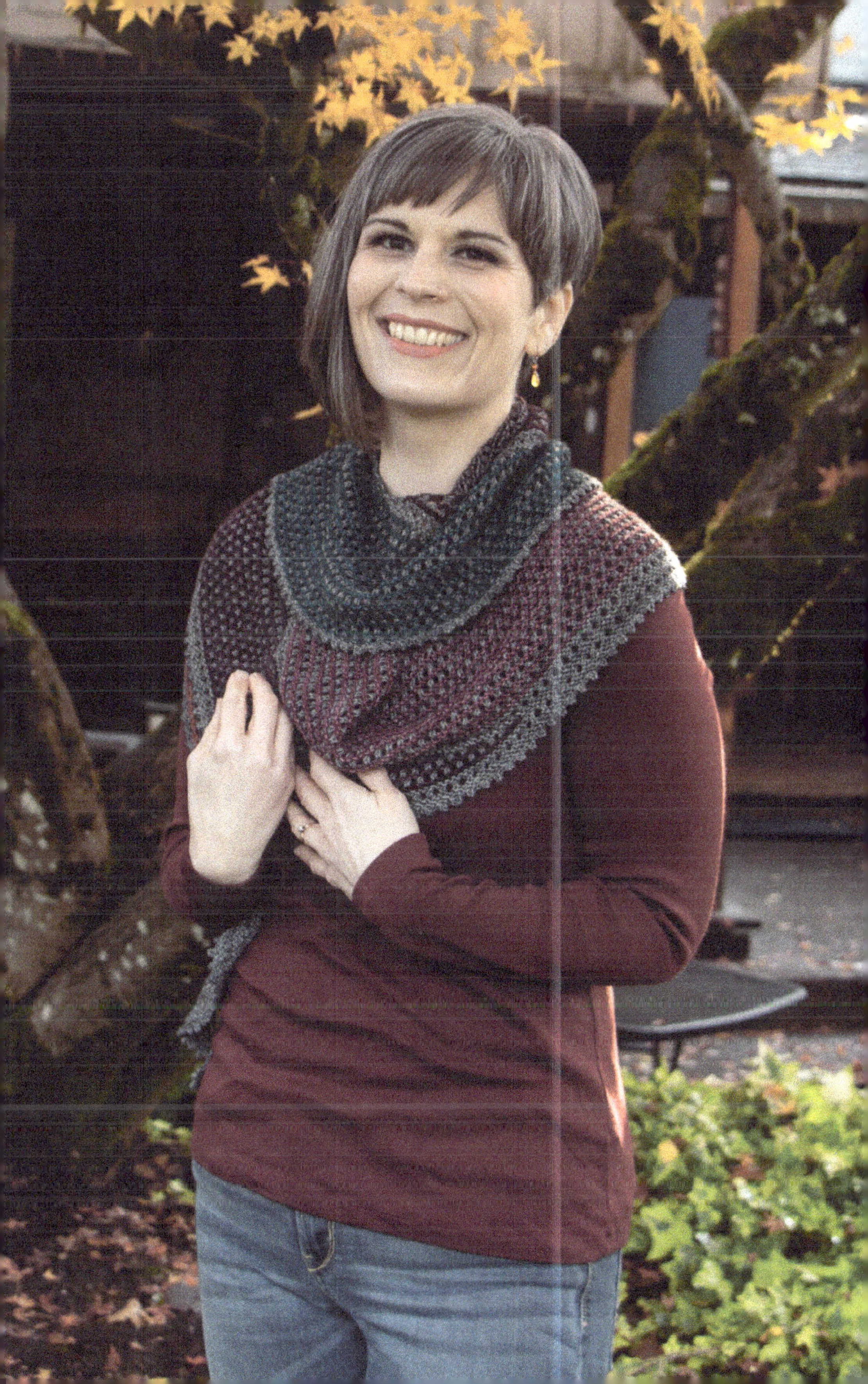

Balance

FINISHED MEASUREMENTS
Wingspan: 82 inches / 208cm
Depth: 9 inches / 23cm

YARN
Fingering Weight: 440 yards / 402m main color, 80 yards / 73m each of
four contrast colors.

Yarn provided by Three Fates Yarn
Aurai Fingering Weight: 70% superwash merino, 20% yak, 10% nylon
Full Skein: 437 yards per 100 grams
Mini Skein: 87 yards / 20 grams

OTHER MATERIALS
US size 6 (4mm) 30 inch / 75cm or larger circular needles, or size needed
to obtain gauge

Tapestry needle

GAUGE
20 sts = 4 inches / 10cm in garter stitch

SPECIAL STITCHES
Cable cast on: Insert the tip of the RH needle between the first and
second sts on LH needle and pull a loop through. Transfer this new
st from the RH needle to the LH needle. Repeat this process until the
required number of new sts have been made.

Knit, yarn over, knit (kyok): Knit, then yo, then knit again into the same
stitch. Three sts made from 1 st.

PATTERN NOTE
Start your next contrast color each time you start a new wedge.

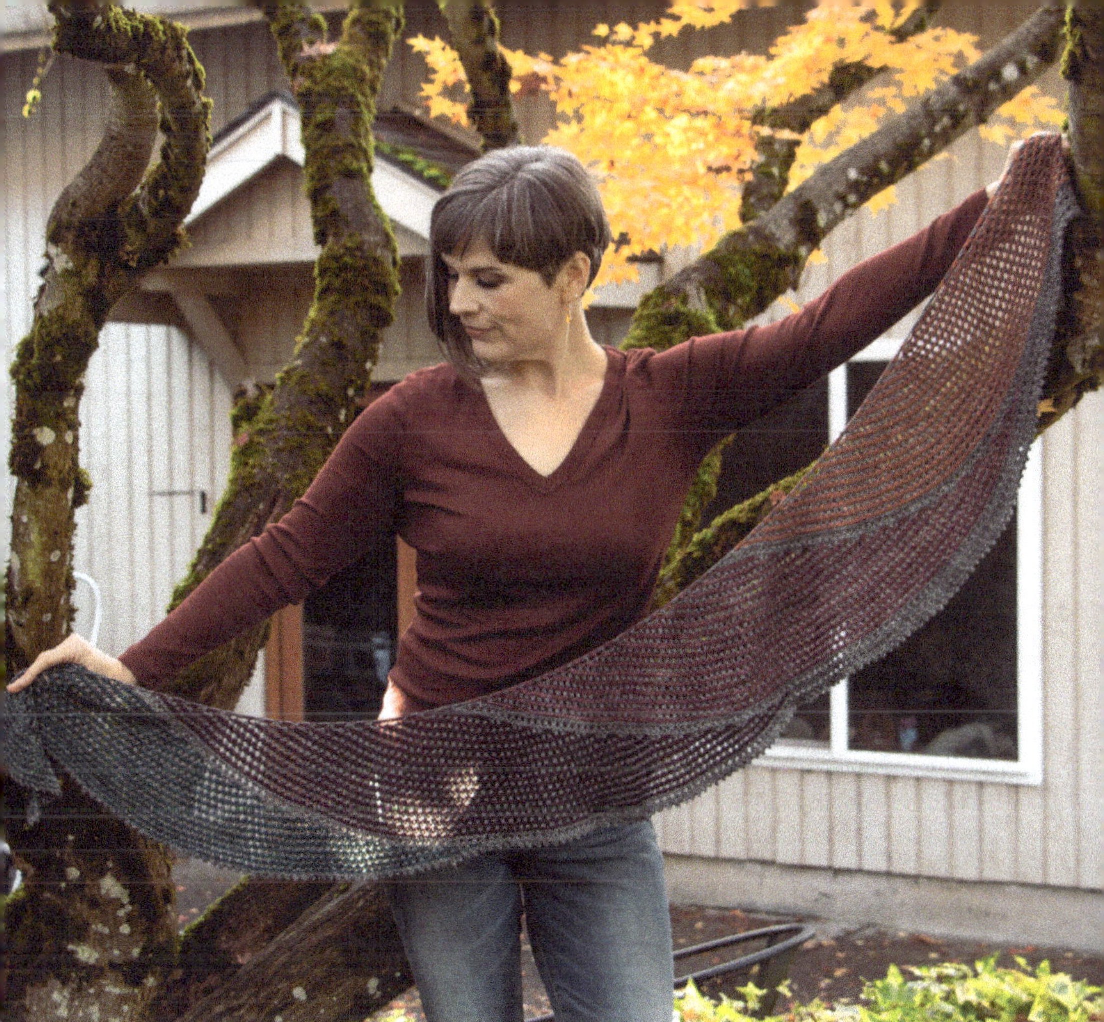

Pattern
Set-Up Wedge
With MC, CO 6 sts and knit one row.
Row 1 (RS): K2, yo, knit to the last 2 sts, yo, k2.
Row 2 (WS): K2, kyok, knit to the last 3 sts, kyok, k2.
Switch to first CC and rep rows 1 and 2 once.
Switch to MC.
Row 3: K2, yo, knit to the last 2 sts, yo, k2.
Row 4: K2, kyok, *yo, p2tog, rep from * to the last 3 sts, kyok, k2.
Switch to first CC.
Row 5: K2, yo, knit to the last 2 sts, yo, k2.
Row 6: K2, kyok, knit to the last 3 sts, kyok, k2.
Rep rows 3 - 6 until you have made 16 CC stripes.
Switch to MC and work rows 5 and 6 once.
Rep rows 3 - 6 one more time using MC.
You will now have 70 yos along the top edge and 216 sts on the needle.

Main Wedge
Switch to next CC.
Row 7: K2, yo, k13, turn.
Row 8: Yo, knit to the last 3 sts, kyok, k2.
Switch to MC.
Row 9: K2, yo, knit to the yo from the start of the previous row, k2tog, k2, turn.
Row 10: Yo, p1, *yo, p2tog, rep from * to the last 3 sts, kyok, k2.
Switch to CC.
Row 11: K2, yo, knit to the yo from the start of the previous row, k2tog, k2, turn.
Row 12: Yo, knit to the last 3 sts, kyok, k2.
Rep rows 9 - 12 until you have made 16 CC stripes.
Switch to MC.
Row 13: K2, yo, knit to the yo from the start of the previous row, k2tog, knit to the last 2 sts, yo, k2.
Row 14: K2, kyok, knit to the last 3 sts, kyok, k2.
3rd rep, stop here and proceed to the bind off.
Row 15: K2, yo, knit to the last 2 sts, yo, k2.
Row 16 (1st rep): K2, kyok, p1, *yo, p2tog, rep from * to the last 3 sts, kyok, k2.
Row 16 (2nd rep): K2, kyok, p1, *yo, p2tog, rep from * to the last 4 sts, p1, kyok, k2.

Row 17: K2, yo, knit to the last 2 sts, yo, k2.
Row 18: K2, kyok, knit to the last 3 sts, kyok, k2.
Rep main wedge section two more times (three reps total).

Picot Bind Off
Step 1: CO 2 sts (using the cable cast on), BO 4 sts.
Step 2: Slip remaining stitch from RH needle back to LH needle.
Rep. steps 1 and 2 until all sts have been bound off.

Weave in ends and block to shape.

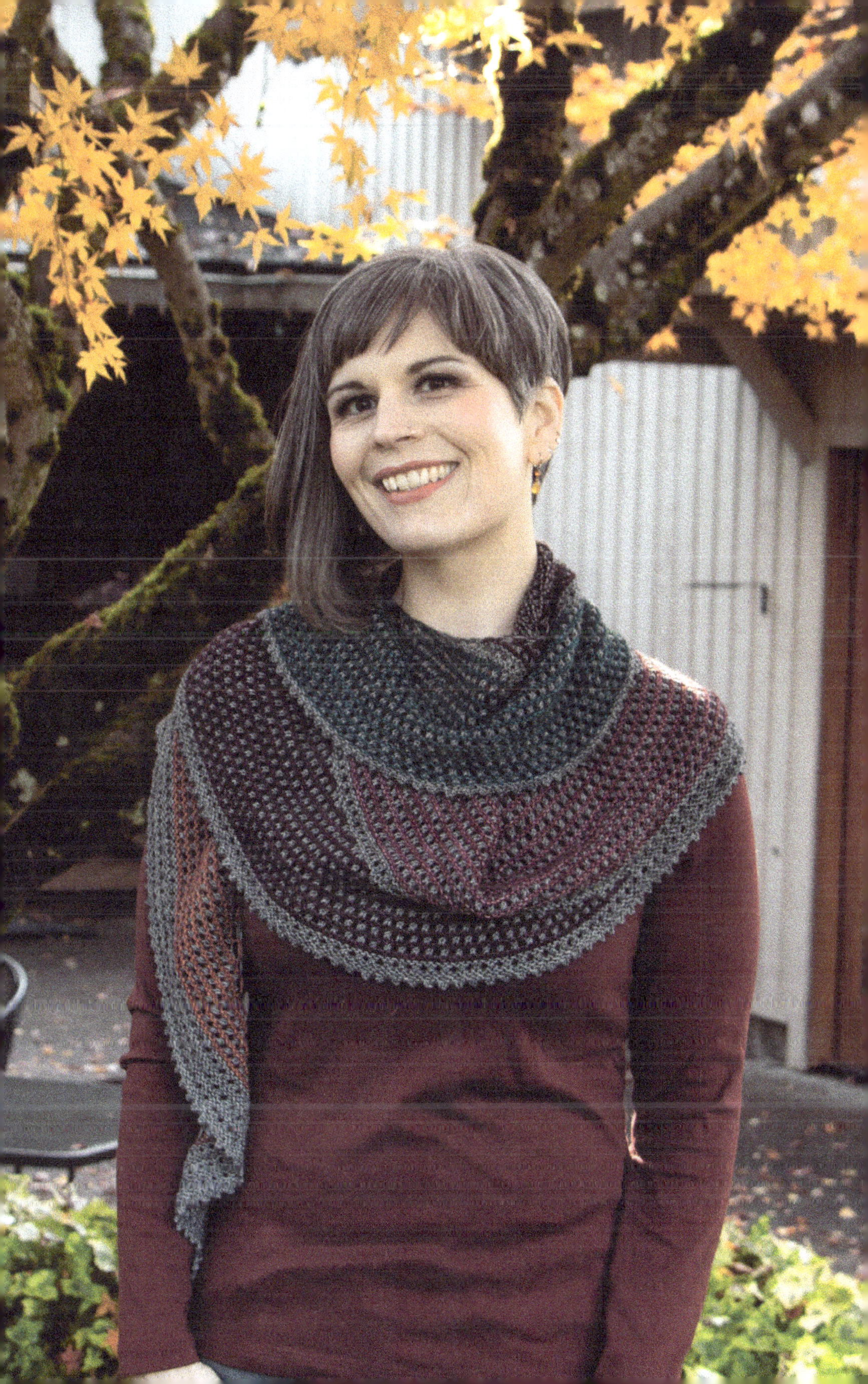

Abstract Fiber

Portland, OR

Lori, owner and operator of Abstract Fiber, creates intense colors with hand painted skeins of yarn and hanks of fiber, one at a time. While she does have a formula for each colorway, each individual skein is its own work of art. One day there may be a little more blue, another day more purple, you never know. That's the thing about independent dyers, even though they have a list of colorways, no two pieces are exactly the same. That's what sets them apart from "Big Wool" that crank out massive dye lots with the same color over and over. While these colors are great for making a solid color sweater, for example, you could add a skein of Abstract Fiber for the yoke! There's enough color for everyone to go around.

These colors are made in Lori's garage-turned-studio at her house in Portland, Oregon. Her clever husband built her shelves and a dye table, and even installed a sink! Now her commute is only a few steps. When Lori is not dyeing, she's knitting, spinning, and teaching online for her local university.

Website: www.abstractfiber.com
Instagram: @abstractfiber
Facebook: Abstract Fiber
Email: abstractfiber@gmail.com

I had the pleasure of attending a virtual meet and greet with Lori last spring. She gave us a tour of her spiffy new studio and spoke about her creative process. She told a very sweet story about her grandparents' courtship that concluded with her grandfather, Harry standing outside her grandmother, Daisy's window singing:
"Daisy, Daisy,
Give me your answer, do!
I'm half crazy,
All for the love of you!
It won't be a stylish marriage,
I can't afford a carriage,
But you'll look sweet on the seat
Of a bicycle built for two!"

The Give Me Your Answer Do mitts were inspired by the story of their courtship and the vibrant yellow and purple yarn that Lori created in their memory.

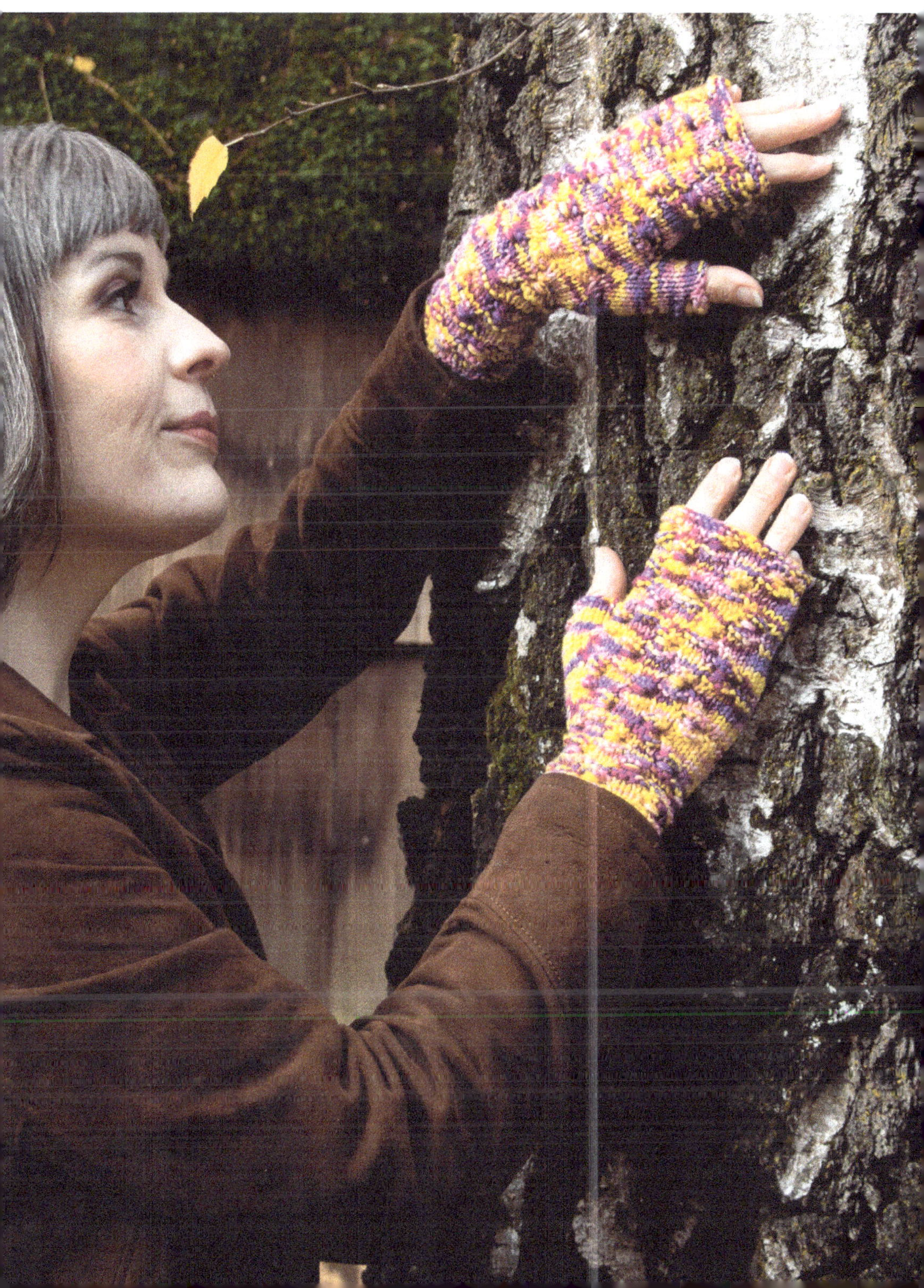

Give Me Your Answer, Do

FINISHED MEASURMENTS
Hand Circumference: 6.5 inches / 16.5cm (with some stretch)
Length: 8.5 inches / 21.5cm (easily adjustable)

YARN
150 yards / 137m of DK weight yarn

Yarn provided by Abstract Fiber
Tahoma: 100% superwash merino
280 yards per 4 oz
Colorway: Harry and Daisy

OTHER MATERIALS
Set of 5 US size 4 (3.5mm) double pointed needles (or circular needle if magic loop is preferred) or size needed to obtain gauge

Stitch holder or scrap yarn

Stitch marker

Tapestry needle

GAUGE
22 sts = 4 inches / 10cm inches in stockinette stitch

SPECIAL STITCHES
Long Knit (lk): Insert the RH needle into the next stitch as to knit, wrap the working yarn around the needle 3 times, and complete the stitch.

Bundle (worked over 5 sts):
Step 1: Slip the next 5 sts to the RH needle dropping the extra wraps and bring the yarn to the front of the work.
Step 2: Slip the 5 sts back to the LH needle and bring the yarn to the back of the work, wrapping the 5 sts.
Rep steps 1 and 2 once more.
Step 3: Slip the 5 sts to the RH needle.
You will now have the working yarn wrapped twice around the 5 elongated sts forming a bundle.

Pattern

Cuff (both mitts)
CO 40 sts and join in the round taking care not to twist the work.
Rnd 1: *K1, p5, k2, rep from * to end of rnd.
Rnd 2: *K1, lk5, k2, rep from * to end of rnd.
Rnd 3: *K1, bundle, k2, rep from * to end of rnd.
Rnd 4: *K1, p5, k2, rep from * to end of rnd.
Rnd 5: Knit to the end of the rnd, knit the first 4 sts of the next rnd. This is the new end of rnd.
Repeat rnds 1 - 5 four more times (five reps total).

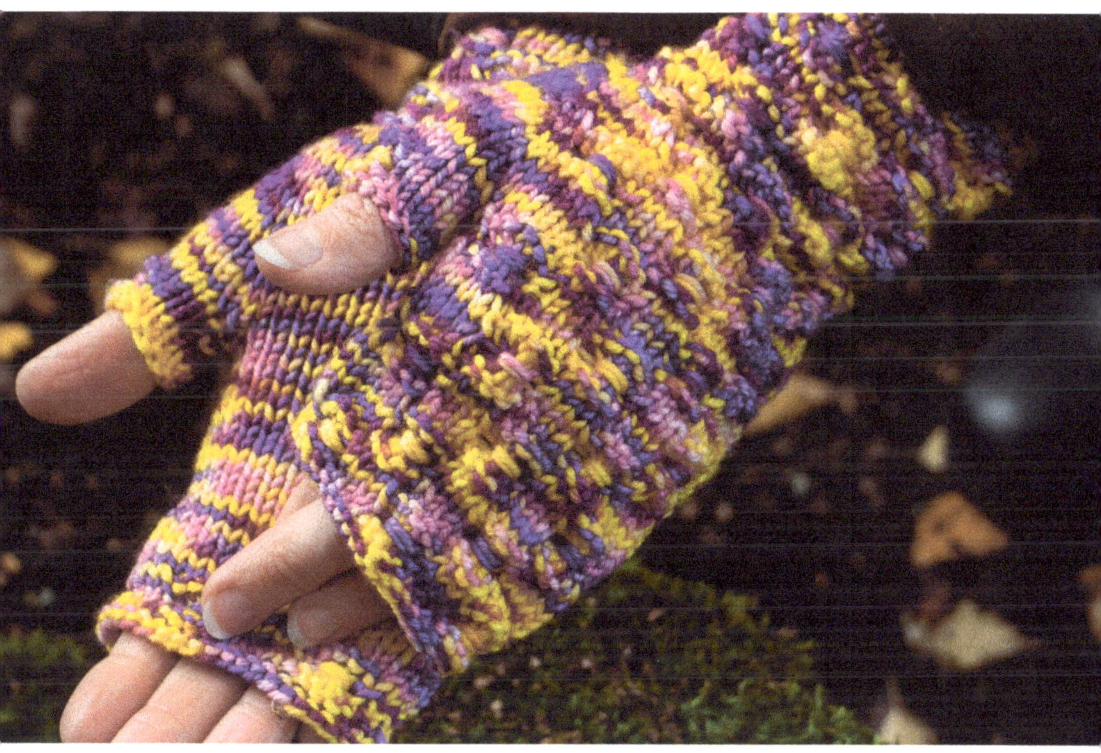

Gusset (right mitt)
Rnd 1: [K1, p5, k2] three times, knit to end of rnd.
Rnd 2: [K1, lk5, k2] twice, k1, lk5, k1, m1, k1, m1, knit to end of rnd.
Rnd 3: [K1, bundle, k2] three times, knit to end of rnd.
Rnd 4: [K1, p5, k2] three times, knit to end of rnd.
Rnd 5: K23, m1, k3, m1, knit to end of rnd.
Rnd 6: K5, [p5, k3] twice, knit to end of rnd.
Rnd 7: K5, [lk5, k3] twice, knit to end of rnd.
Rnd 8: K5, [bundle, k3] twice, k2, m1, k5, m1, knit to end of rnd.
Rnd 9: K5, [p5, k3] twice, knit to end of rnd.
Rnd 10: Knit.

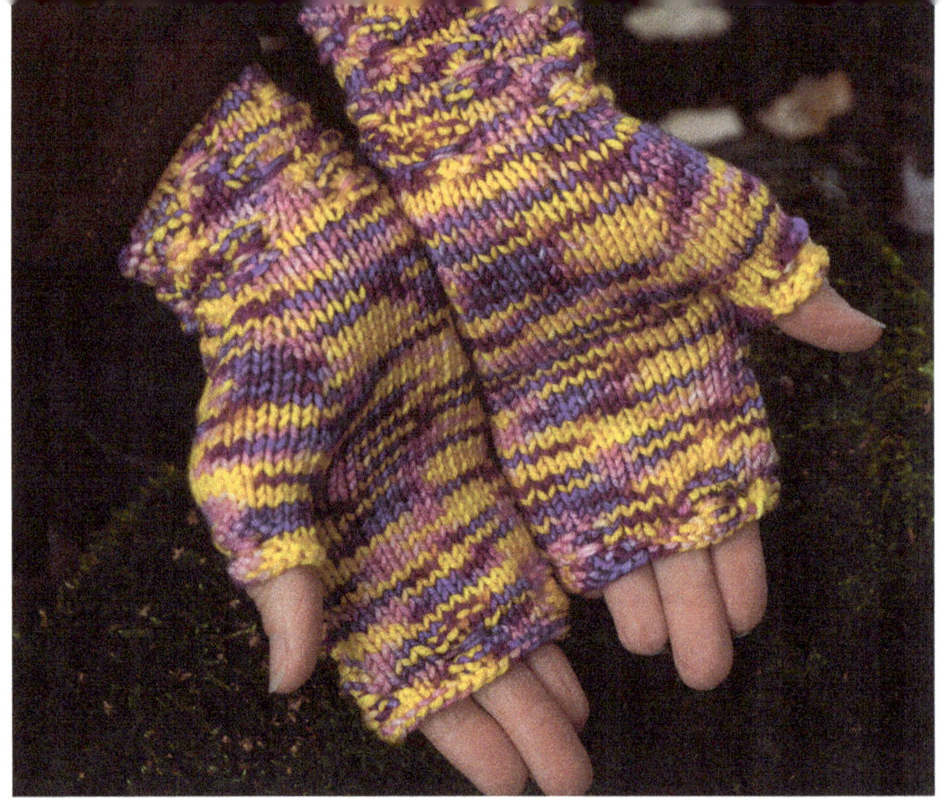

Rnd 11: [K1, p5, k2] twice, k1, p5, k1, m1, k7, m1, knit to end of rnd.
Rnd 12: [K1, lk5, k2] three times, knit to end of rnd.
Rnd 13: [K1, bundle, k2] three times, knit to end of rnd.
Rnd 14: [K1, p5, k2] twice, k1, p5, k1, m1, k9, m1, knit to end of rnd.
Rnd 15: Knit.
Rnd 16: K5, [p5, k3] twice, knit to end of rnd.
Rnd 17: K5, [lk5, k3] twice, k2, m1, k11, m1, knit to end of rnd.
Rnd 18: K5, [bundle, k3] twice, knit to end of rnd.
Rnd 19: K5, [p5, k3] twice, knit to end of rnd.
Rnd 20: K23, place next 13 sts on a holder or scrap yarn, using the
backward loop CO 1 st, knit to end of rnd.

Gusset (left mitt)
Rnd 1: [K1, p5, k2] three times, knit to end of rnd.
Rnd 2: [K1, lk5, k2] three times, knit to last st, m1, k1, m1.
Rnd 3: [K1, bundle, k2] three times, knit to end of rnd.
Rnd 4: [K1, p5, k2] three times, knit to end of rnd.
Rnd 5: Knit to last 3 sts, m1, k3, m1.
Rnd 6: K5, [p5, k3] twice, knit to end of rnd.
Rnd 7: K5, [lk5, k3] twice, knit to end of rnd.
Rnd 8: K5, [bundle, k3] twice, knit to last 5 sts, m1, k5, m1.
Rnd 9: K5, [p5, k3] twice, knit to end of rnd.
Rnd 10: Knit.

Rnd 11: [K1, p5, k2] twice, knit to last 7 sts, m1, k7, m1.
Rnd 12: [K1, lk5, k2] three times, knit to end of rnd.
Rnd 13: [K1, bundle, k2] three times, knit to end of rnd.
Rnd 14: [K1, p5, k2] three times, knit to last 9 sts, m1, k9, m1.
Rnd 15: Knit.
Rnd 16: K5, [p5, k3] twice, knit to end of rnd.
Rnd 17: K5, [lk5, k3] twice, knit to last 11 sts, m1, k11, m1.
Rnd 18: K5, [bundle, k3] twice, knit to end of rnd.
Rnd 19: K5, [p5, k3] twice, knit to end of rnd.
Rnd 20: Knit to the last 13 sts, place next 13 sts on a holder or scrap yarn, using the backward loop CO 1 st.

Hand (both mitts)
Rnd 1: [K1, p5, k2] three times, knit to end of rnd.
Rnd 2: [K1, lk5, k2] three times, knit to end of rnd.
Rnd 3: [K1, bundle, k2] three times, knit to end of rnd.
Rnd 4: [K1, p5, k2] three times, knit to end of rnd.
Rnd 5: Knit.
Rnd 6: K5, [p5, k3] twice, knit to end of rnd.
Rnd 7: K5, [lk5, k3] twice, knit to end of rnd.
Rnd 8: K5, [bundle, k3] twice, knit to end of rnd.
Rnd 9: K5, [p5, k3] twice, knit to end of rnd.
Rnd 10: Knit.
Repeat rnds 1 - 10 once more (two reps total)
Rnd 11: *K1, p5, k2, rep from * to end of rnd.
Rnd 12: *K1, lk5, k2, rep from * to end of rnd.
Rnd 13: *K1, bundle, k2, rep from * to end of rnd.
Rnd 14: *K1, p5, k2, rep from * to end of rnd.
BO all sts loosely purlwise. (Purl each st before binding it off.)

Thumb (both mitts)
Place the 13 sts from the holder onto the needle. Pick up and knit 3 sts from the cast on edge at the hand.
Rnd 1: Sl1, pm (this is the end of rnd), k11, ssk, k1, k2tog.
Rnds 2 - 4: Knit.
Rnd 5: K3, p5, knit to end of rnd.
Rnd 6: K3, lk5, knit to end of rnd.
Rnd 7: K3, bundle, knit to end of rnd.
Rnd 8: K3, p5, knit to end of rnd.
BO all sts loosely purlwise. (Purl each st before binding it off.)

Weave in ends and block to shape.

Silver Falls Fiber Co.
Silverton, OR

Silver Falls Fiber Company is owned by Leann Bleakney, a third-generation Oregonian whose family still lives on the Silverton farm her grandfather established. Her grandmother taught her to knit when she was a small girl. Leann's mother still has the first thing Leann ever knit: a seven foot long scarf with holes in it as big as your head. Growing up on a farm with sheep (Suffolk) confirmed her devotion to all things fiber.

Leann was an exchange student in Norway in high school and in college. Everybody knits in Norway, and Leann came home truly dedicated to knitting. She now knits every single day and has for more than three decades. About five years ago a friend got her started spinning, and now she tries to do that most days as well. Leann jokes that she is basically just backing up through the process: from knitting to spinning the yarn to dyeing the yarn to knit and fiber to spin. She has thought about taking yet another step back into the process and getting sheep on the family farm. Some day she just might.

Leann's dyeing inspiration comes from Oregon. She is enthralled by the palette of colors that our state, and even the just the Willamette Valley, has to offer. She is constantly awed by the color she sees on the farm, in the valley, and in her travels.

Website coming soon: www.silverfallsfiber.com
Email: lbleakney@gmail.com

Butterfly Fiber and Farm

Salem, OR

Tonie was born and raised outside of Portland, Oregon, and started hand dyeing yarn and fiber a couple of years ago. Her creations can be found on Etsy through her business, Butterfly Fiber. Tonie is passionate about vibrant colors, and enjoys coming up with unique colorways and blends. She blames her dyeing addiction on her friend Leann of Silver Falls Fiber Co. When Tonie isn't in her dye studio, she is running a printing business and taking care of her animals on her Salem farm.

Shop: www.etsy.com/shop/ButterflyFiber
Email: butterflyfiberfarm@gmail.com

Toni and Leann teamed up to provide me with yarn for a large scale project. They both worked from the same photo of a blackberry patch with Tonie creating the variegated colors and Leann the subtle semi-solids.

I was inspired by Tonie and Leann's friendship and collaboration to create a pattern that combined their yarns seamlessly. The result, as is often the case with a good friendship, is something big, beautiful, and very comfortable.

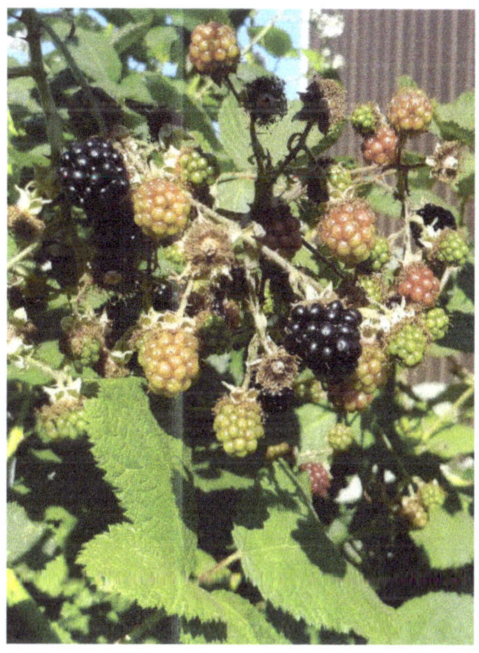

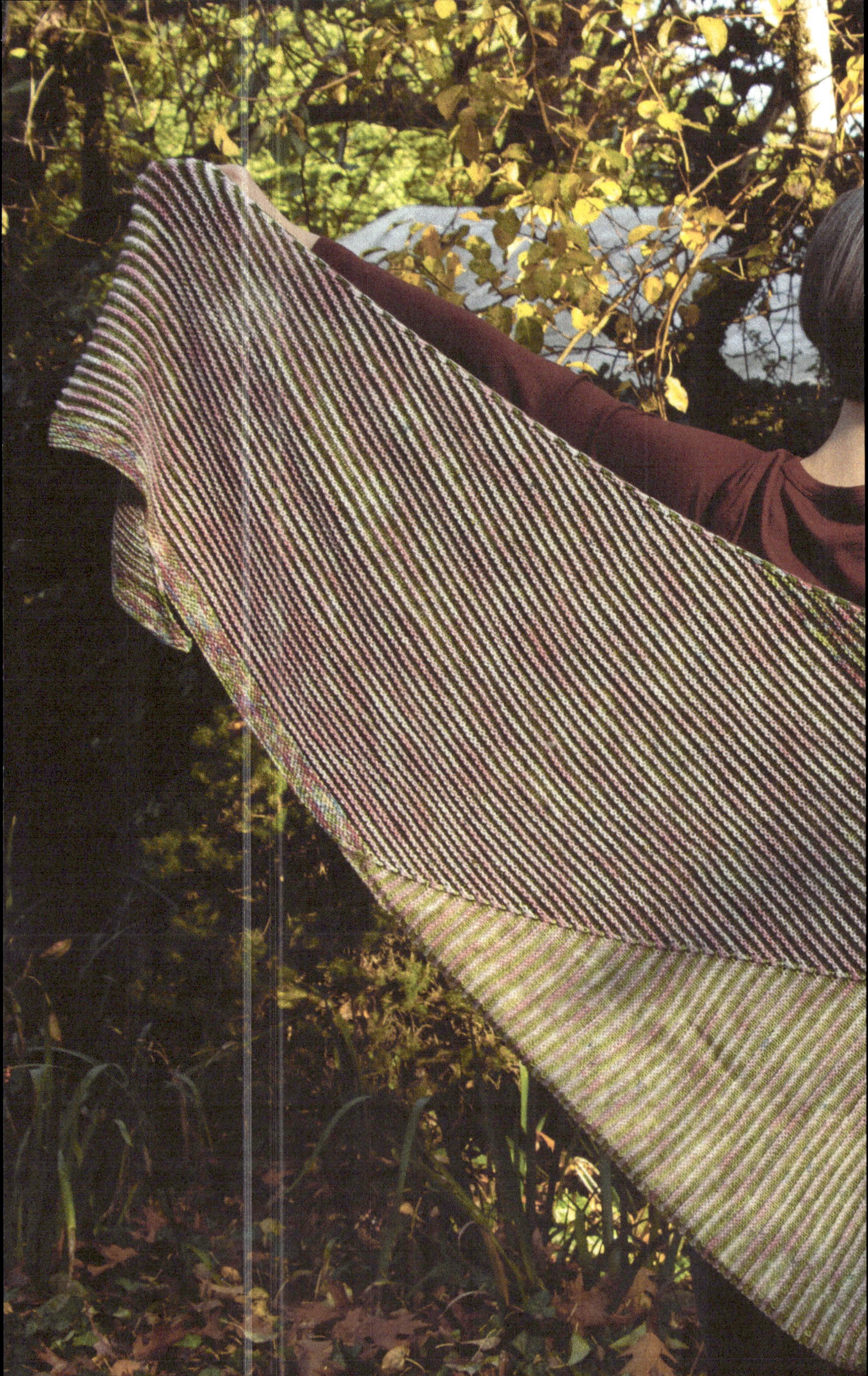

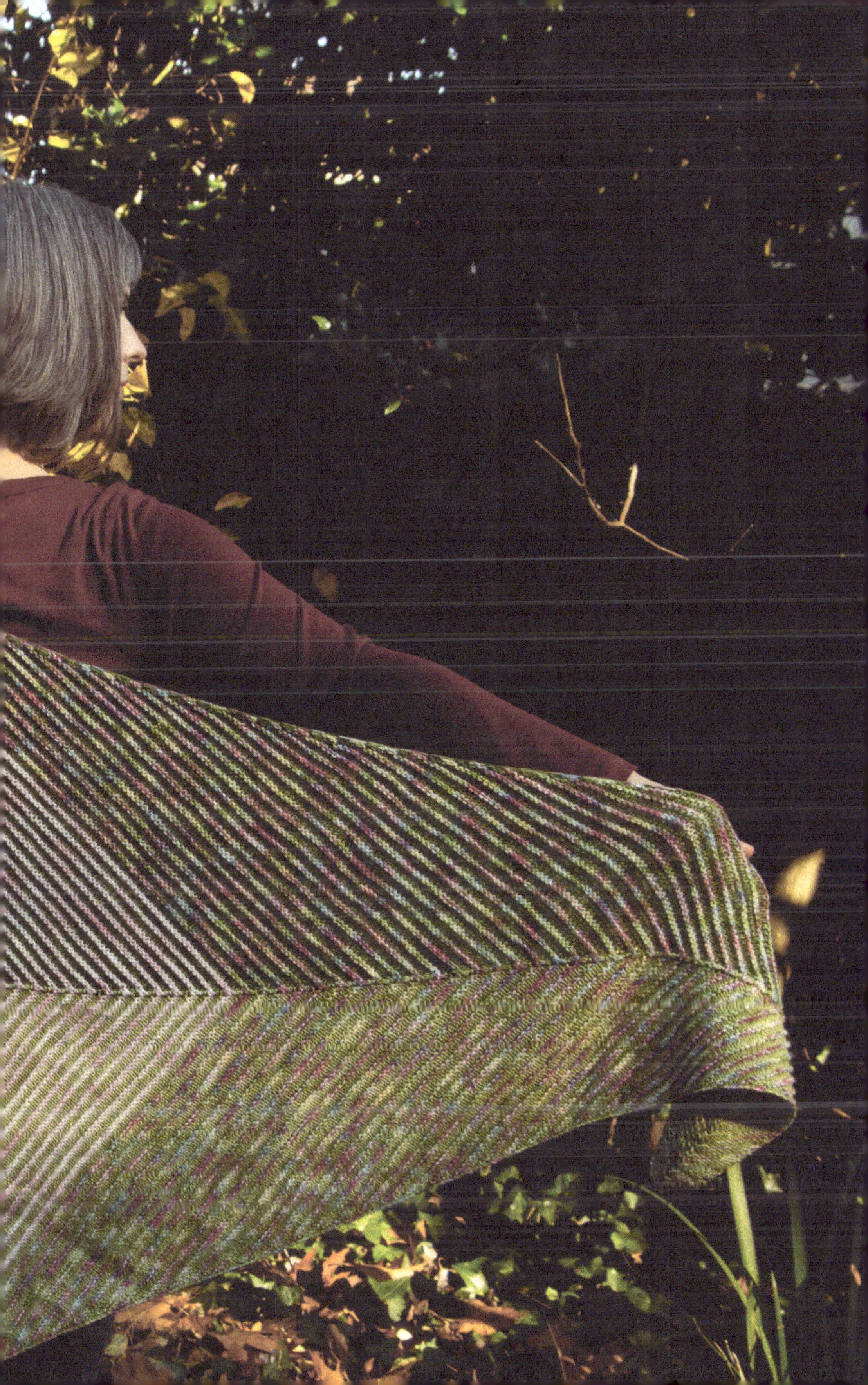

Berry Patch

Finished Measurments (as shown)
Wingspan: 90 inches / 229cm
Depth: 27 inches / 69cm

Yarn
Fingering weight yarn in the following amounts:
A: 290 yards / 265m
B: 430 yards / 393m
C: 220 yards / 201m
D: 430 yards / 393m

The pattern is written using percentages of yarn used so be sure to weigh your yarns before starting. You can use any size skeins you want, just know that the finished size will vary with the size of your skeins. You will use nearly all of colors B and D, so calculations should be based on the size of those skeins. The simplest way to go is to use 4 equal sized skeins.

Yarn provided by Silver Falls Fiber Co.
Fingering: 80% superwash merino, 20% nylon
434 yards per 120g
Colorways: Raspberry Leaves (C) and Blackberry Leaves (B)
Yarn provided by Butterfly Fiber and Farm
Fingering: 80% superwash merino, 20% nylon
434 yards per 120g
Colorways: In the Berry Patch (A) and Starting to Ripen (D)

Other Materials
US size 6 (4mm) 30 inch / 75cm or larger circular needle or size needed to obtain gauge

Removable stitch marker

Tapestry needle

Gauge
22 sts = 4 inches / 10cm in garter stitch

Special Stitches
Central Double Decrease (cdd): Sl2 sts together knitwise, k1, sl the 2 slipped sts over the knit st.

Pattern Note
A central double decrease is worked on all RS rows creating a central spine. The stitch at the center of the spine is called the center stitch and will be used as a landmark in the knitting.

When switching yarns in the center of the row be sure to leave the yarn hanging in the back of the work.

Pattern
Set Up
With yarn A, CO 5 sts.
Row 1 (RS): K1, kfb, k1, kfb, k1.
Row 2 (WS): Knit.
Row 3: K1, kfb, cdd, kfb, k1.
Row 4: K1, kfb, k3, kfb, k1.
Row 5: K1, kfb, k1, cdd, k1, kfb, k1.
Row 6: K1, kfb, k5, kfb, k1.
You should now be able to see the center spine forming. You can use a removable stitch marker to mark the center stitch. (Do not use a standard on-the-needle marker as it will get in the way of your cdd.)

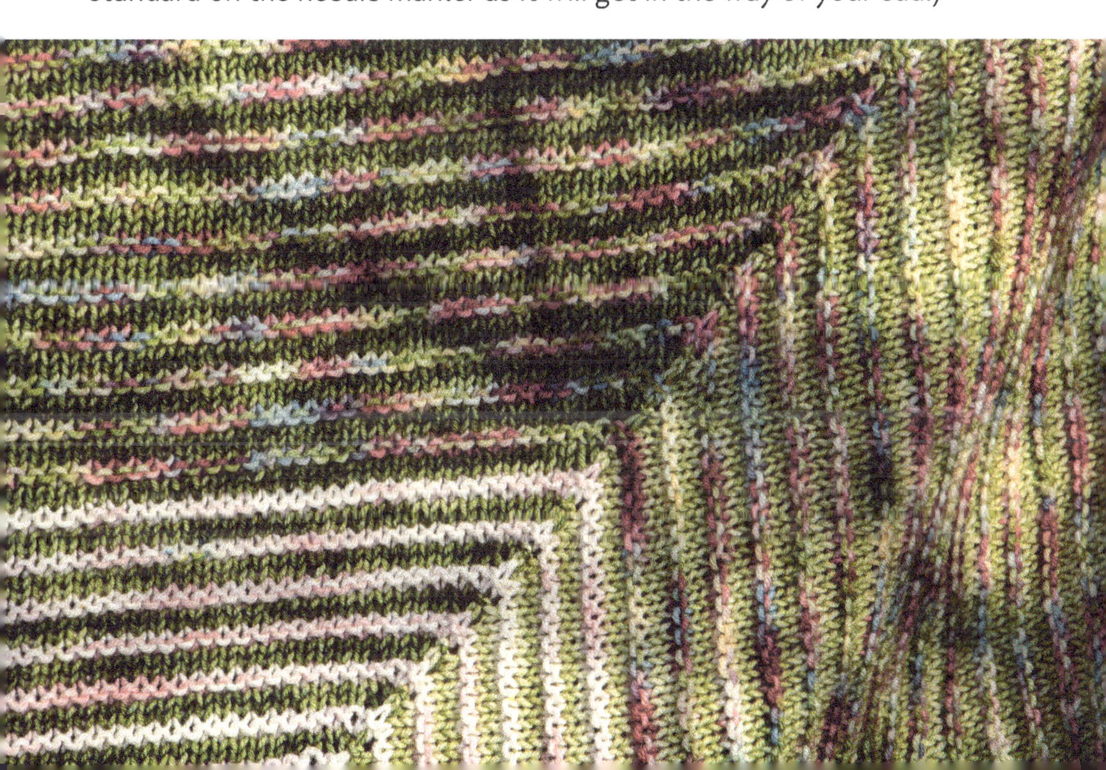

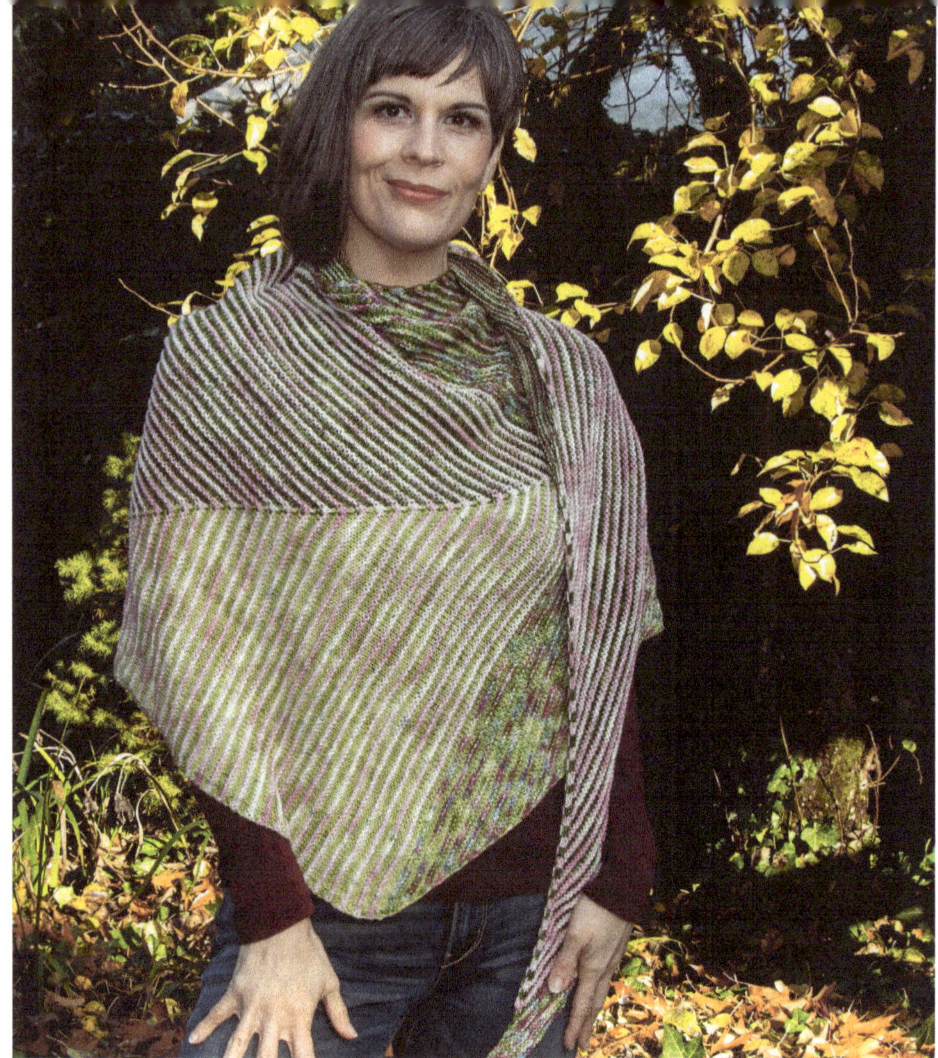

Section A

Row 7: With color B, k1, kfb, knit to 1 st before the center st, ccd, with color C, knit to last 2 sts, kfb, k1.

Row 8: With color C, k1, kfb, purl to center st, knit center st, with color B, purl to last 2 sts, kfb, k1.

With color A

Row 9: K1, kfb, knit to 1 st before the center st, ccd, knit to last 2 sts, kfb, k1.

Row 10: K1, kfb, knit to last 2 sts, kfb, k1.

Rep rows 7 - 10 until you've used half of color A and a quarter of colors B and C.

Cut color A leaving a 6 - 8 inch / 15 - 20cm tail.

Section B

Row 11: With color B, k1, kfb, knit to 1 st before the center st, ccd, with color C, knit to end of row.

Row 12: With color C, k3, purl to center st, purl center st, with color B, purl to last 2 sts, kfb, k1.
With color D
Row 13: K1, kfb, knit to 1 st before the center st, ccd, knit to end of row.
Row 14: Knit to last 2 sts, kfb, k1.
Rep rows 11 - 14 until 8 sts remain to the left of the center stitch. (If you are running short of yarn you can move to the end section earlier. Just be sure to complete one final rep of rows 11 and 12 before moving on.)
Rep rows 11 and 12 once more.

End
With color A
Row 15: K1, kfb, knit to 1 st before the center st, ccd, knit to end of row.
Row 16: Knit to last 2 sts, kfb, k1.
Rep rows 15 and 16 until only 1 sts remains to the left of the center stitch.
Rep row 15 once more.
BO all stitches loosely.
Weave in ends and block to shape.

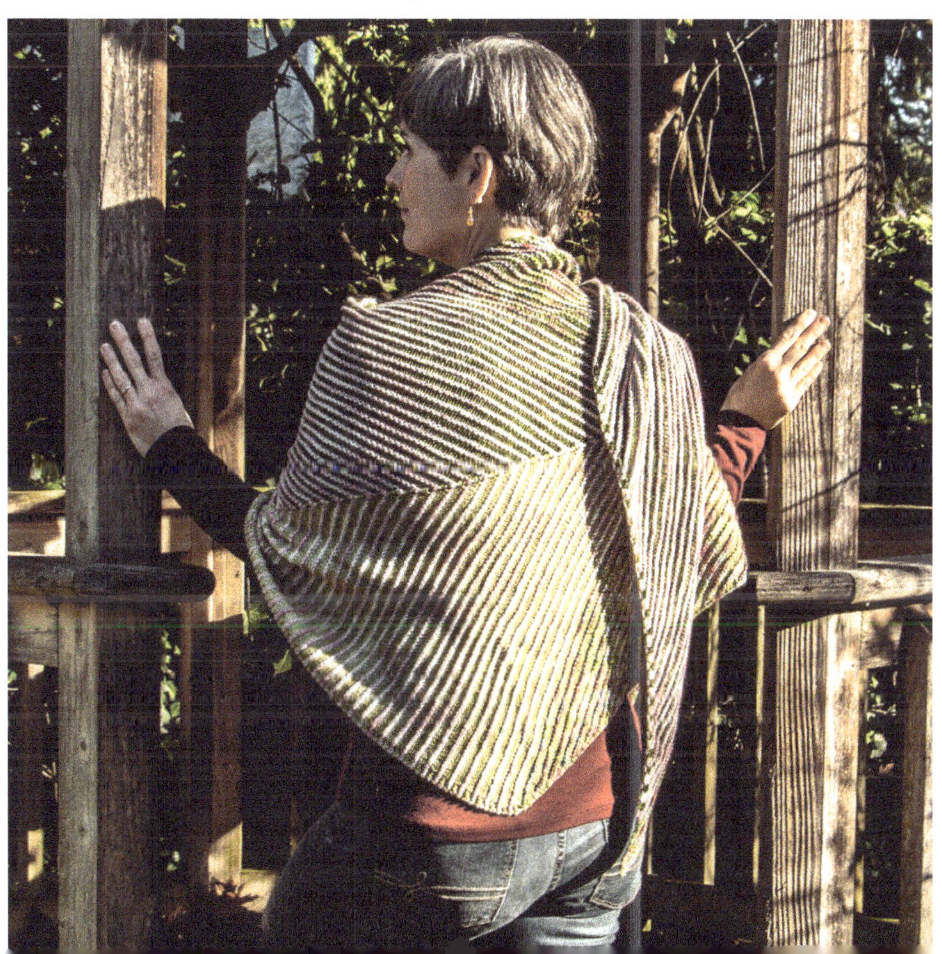

Acknowledgments

This book would not have happened without the help, support, and contributions of the following folks. Thank you!

To Stephen Gerken, my husband and my editor, thank you for agreeing to do this with me, again! And thank you for knowing which hat I needed you to wear on any given day.

To Marilyn Barnes, my photographer and my friend, thanks for being both.

To my lovely model, Reba Sparrow, thanks for being your amazing self!

To my test knitters, Marilyn Barnes, Su Fennern, Heather Hagen, Kendra Meinert Hodson, Barbara Holland, Jan Just, Michele A. Ray, Dawn Rosiejka, Eva Schweber, Renata Suzuki, Margaret Weddell, and Kim Williams, thanks for your care and attention to detail.

To the dyers who provided yarn, thank you for believing in me and this project. It wouldn't have happened without your generosity and support.

To all my Kickstarter donors, thank you for taking the plunge and supporting this project.

Cast and Crew

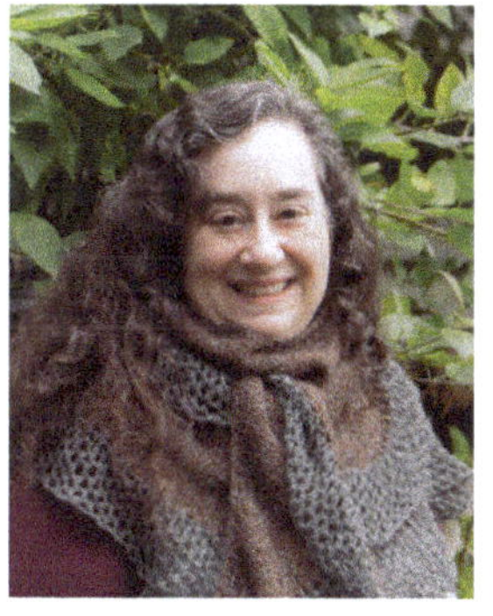

AUTHOR Theressa Silver is a freelance designer, teacher, and author of *Knitting Wild* and *Crescents*. She has designed for magazines including *Jane Austen Knits* and *Enchanted Knits*. She is a contributor to the Knit Picks Independent Designers Program. She also has an assortment of self-published patterns available on Ravelry under the name ArgentGal Designs. Theressa is a biologist by training and the influence of math and science can be seen in many of her designs. When she is not knitting she likes to be outside kayaking or hiking. She has been known to stop on the trail, stare at something for a bit, and then exclaim, "I bet I could knit that!" She lives in Milwaukie, OR with her husband, two cats, and a dog, all of whom occasionally participate one way or another in the knitting process.

PHOTOGRAPHER Marilyn Barnes began taking photos when her grandchildren were born and quickly developed an interest in nature photography. A self-professed "details person," she has a wonderful eye for texture and color and takes spectacular close-ups of plants and animals, many of which she sells as note cards. Over the years some of her favorite subjects, besides her grandchildren, have included roses, birds, butterflies, and dragonflies. A knitter of fifty years, when she isn't behind the lens of a camera, she's likely to have a pair of knitting needles in her hands. Marilyn lives in Milwaukie, OR and can be found riding her bike around town with her camera safely tucked in her saddle bag.

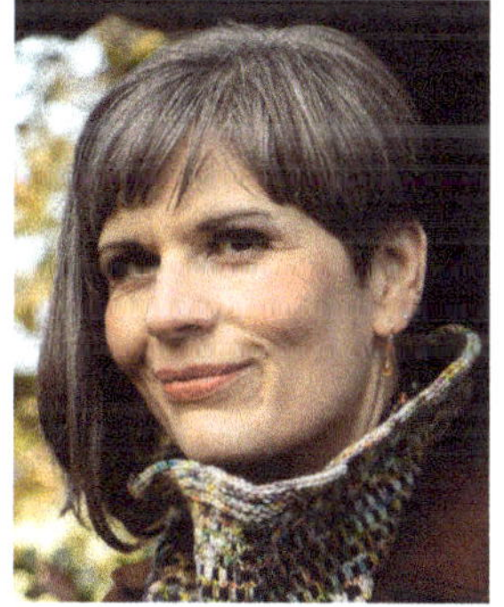

MODEL Reba Sparrow is the Executive Producer and story coach for The Mystery Box Show (mysteryboxshow.com and @mysteryboxpdx), a voice over artist, and a model based in Portland. Follow her on Instagram (@happyapplepdx) and Facebook (@rebasparrow). Trust me, you'll be glad you did!